In Deepest Appreciation
for all the Great Teachers that have
Lit the Way

We Join in Love and Peace
Because of You

TABLE OF CONTENTS

FOREWORD

By Lisa Natoli – Author of "Gorgeous for God"

There is tremendous power in commitment when it is combined with a little willingness to have your life transformed by deliberate acts of forgiveness. In every situation, no matter how difficult, you can choose Love. You can decide to be happy instead of angry. You can choose joy instead of depression. You can allow every encounter to be a new opportunity to know yourself as God created you: all light.

It is a great privilege for me to write the foreword to Robyn Busfield's beautiful book, *Forgiveness is the Home of Miracles*. I love this book for several reasons but mostly because I am reminded of the time when I first began practicing *A Course in Miracles* back in 1992. My deepest desire was to meet people (spiritual companions) who were walking the same path as me, and who could, by their own demonstration, show me how to incorporate the lessons of forgiveness and faith into my own daily life.

Robyn Busfield is such a companion.

Forgiveness is the Home of Miracles is Robyn's personal experience through the 365 Workbook lessons of *A Course in Miracles*.

I remember my own initial reaction when I first heard of *A Course in Miracles:* sheer excitement. I was thrilled by the possibility of miracles occurring in my life. Then I had a different reaction when I stood in the Barnes and Noble bookstore on Astor Place in Manhattan, flipping through the pages of *A Course in Miracles,* contemplating whether or not to pay $35 for a book: confusion and a feeling of being completely overwhelmed. I tried to read a few paragraphs and not a single sentence made any sense to me. What does it mean, "There is no world" and that "God's Will for me is perfect happiness?"

These were completely foreign ideas in my life of failed relationships, addiction, and constant worrying. I couldn't conceive of an experience of consistent joy and peace which is exactly what Jesus, the author of *A Course in Miracles,* promises. And yet, there was something else that stirred within me. There was a feeling that this book was the answer to all my prayers. So I bought it, took it home, and promptly put it on my bookshelf where it sat collecting dust for the next five years.

Occasionally, when I was in really deep fear or needed a miracle, I would drag the blue book off the shelf and flip through the pages trying to find a solution. I treated it like a book of magic and alchemy.

What happened next can only be described as Divine Grace: I started meeting people who studied and practiced *A Course in Miracles.* These people were "practicing the Workbook lessons" and not just picking up the book when they were in despair. These people had made a commitment to go through all 365 Workbook lessons in an effort to see their lives transformed. It was through watching them on their daily path that gave me the courage to begin applying the principles of *A Course in Miracles* in my own life.

The result: I started feeling really happy. My relationships improved. I noticed I no longer got sick. Fear disappeared and was replaced with a renewed joy for living.

I am grateful to Robyn for letting us take a peek inside her life while she took this journey through the Workbook lessons, which can often appear messy and chaotic. She allows us to see her in vulnerable moments, in fear, in uncertainty, in confusion, and just as quickly, she shows us the miracle of healing that occurs as she applies the Workbook lessons to the situation and "problems" in her life.

The thing that struck me most as I was reading through Robyn's thoughts and questions, as she applied the Workbook lessons in her life, was THE SPEED by which she was able to get herself right back on track to thinking with God. To me, this is more important than always saying the right thing or always trying to be good and holy.

Robyn allows us to see her stumble and fall as she moves back and forth between illusion and Heaven, but she is always herself: lovable, adorable, authentic, and sincere. I think it's valuable to have a teacher who is figuring things out, showing her mistakes, and one who wonders aloud, "What is the point of all this?"—in essence, someone who is just like us!

This book you are holding in your hands is an inside glimpse into one woman's mind who had the courage to use her own life as a demonstration of the healing power of "forgiveness." This book offers many great practical examples revealing that no matter how difficult it gets in any situation you can choose another way of thinking; you can choose Love instead of grievances.

You'll be delighted to find how easy it is to choose Love.

Love Lisa

By Lisa Natoli - Author of "Gorgeous for God"

Miracles are examples of right thinking,
aligning your perceptions with truth
as God created it.

- A Course in Miracles

Chapter 1

A Shift in Perception

THE LIGHT BETWEEN THE GAPS

It is August 2007. I have been studying the "Magnetic Laws of the Universe" for more than a decade. Acknowledging and implementing these unquestionable laws over all these years has indeed brought harmonious changes to my once questionable life.

However, little did I know my world was about to change. My perception was about to be questioned yet again. And just when I thought I had it all figured out...

On this warm August day in Redondo Beach, California, I sit to visualize as I had done for many years after discovering the knowledge of the now famous *Law of Attraction*. I have become very good at utilizing the Law of Attraction and making it work in my life. This day I am visualizing with the intent to manifest a positive outcome for my recently published book. I have been visualizing for just a few minutes when I hear this gentle Inner Voice—the Inner Voice I have come to know very well at this point in my life. It gently said, "We are not going to let the Universe know what we want today. We are not going to manifest the outcome of your book. Instead, we will be silent and allow a Higher Knowing to offer the best outcome. In fact, we are going to allow a Higher Knowing to offer the best outcome for *every* event and circumstance in your life from this day forward."

I was floored. For many years, each time I visualized, I had received strong, encouraging, passionate feelings. It *always* felt like the right thing to do. Now, I was getting the message that this was no longer the right thing to do! I knew I trusted my best friend within—my Higher Self. How could I ignore my best friend today when I had paid close attention to it for so many years and knew it had *always* been right?

I felt that there could only be one reason why this change was occurring in my life. I had recently begun to study and practice the principles of a Text and Workbook called *A Course in Miracles*. Also referred to and known as *the Course*, or *ACIM*. A friend had given me this rather large and biblical looking book a few years earlier. At the time I read a little more than half the Text, each page at least four times over to assist in understanding this unique verbiage, and then placed this somewhat complicated book back upon the shelf.

Recently, after picking up the Course once again and thumbing through it, I felt a desire to begin the lessons. There are 365 lessons in the Workbook of the Course, one lesson for each day of the year. There is no set rule to doing the lessons, only that I am urged not to attempt to complete more than one lesson in a day.

I have been told that once you partake in the lessons unusual events begin to occur. Apparently, from what I understand, conflicting thoughts that take place in the wrong mind surface for healing. I am only a couple of weeks into the lessons and so far not much has unfolded in relation to unusual or uncomfortable events, yet a noticeable shift in the everyday guidance I am receiving has occurred. The guidance I received while visualizing is one such example.

After visualizing for so many years, I found it difficult to just stop. It had become a big part of my life. I also wasn't completely sold on this new idea of not visualizing. So the next morning I sit to visualize once again. It didn't take long, seconds maybe, before the same Inner Voice led me away from visualizing and gently guided me to hand all outcomes over to a Higher Knowing.

Okay, I didn't need any more convincing. This August day of 2007 would be the last day I would sit to visualize. I don't feel this means that I don't have a say in what I desire to see around me. After exploring the possibility of creation, I have come to understand that whatever I see and enjoy will continue to be. Or whatever I give little focus toward, or desire for, will cease to exist. I know this much: I am not going to walk around with my eyes closed. So, my ability to create a desired environment will continue to be based upon my enjoyment of my surroundings. I think this is the catch: Don't control the outcome by placing *emphasis* on the outcome. It's like the saying, "Let go, let God," Or, "Jesus take the wheel." I hand over the controls to my future, because I believe there is a *Higher Knowing* that knows better than me. Then as I move forward, I move in the direction that I am gently guided to, while enjoying whatever I choose to enjoy along the way.

I feel that relaxation is a big key in all of this. I find at times I take the wheel back without realizing that I am taking it back. This seems to happen when I am feeling nervous and uncomfortable. It also seems to happen when I feel uncertain that a Higher Knowing will make the right choice for me.

Okay, so in this moment, right now, I *ask* to relax and have faith in handing the wheel over to a Higher Knowing. I also *ask* to hear and trust that this Higher Knowing knows better than me. So first, I must practice relaxing. Second, I must practice listening. And third, I must practice my faith in this Higher Knowing.

WHERE DID ACIM COME FROM?

Since commencing this journey with ACIM, I have spent time considering Jesus' teachings and His spoken link with ACIM. When I initially read ACIM a number of years ago, on more than one occasion, I actually felt the words were coming directly from Jesus. It was a couple of years later when I was talking to a student of ACIM and he said, "Oh do you know who instructed Helen Schucman to scribe the Course? I asked, "Who?" He said, "Jesus!"

Recently, I have watched a number of ACIM interviews. In a conversation with Bill Thetford, Helen Schucman nervously explained that the Voice which came to her for the scribing had identified Himself as Jesus. Also, in these interviews, teachers and students state their belief that Jesus was in fact the Voice which instructed Helen Schucman to take notes as they were offered, thus completing a manuscript of 1,200 plus pages, comprising of the Text, Workbook, Manual for Teaches, and Clarification of Terms. Additional material which Helen Schucman also scribed and was noted as an extension to the Course is, "The Song of Prayer – Prayer, Forgiveness, Healing" and "Psychotherapy: Purpose, Process and Practice" (this additional material is included in the Third Edition of ACIM, headed "Supplements").

Due to Jesus' message of 2000 years ago being partly destroyed and partly altered, could it be true that He has come forward to relay the original message again? That is quite the question. But what is the answer? The answer, I believe, can only be found within each reader's heart.

A VISIT TO THE HOLY LAND

Going back in time, a decade to be exact, it is summer of 97 and I find myself laying on the beautiful white sands of Manhattan Beach in California. I am engrossed in a book. This book bares many quotes from the bible which are having quite an impact on me. As I read the words something shifts in me. This book causes me, for the first time in my life, to stop and consider Jesus' true existence 2000 years earlier.

I had never been religious. In fact, if anyone said the words, God, Jesus, Holy Spirit, etc., I would feel very uncomfortable. Not that I didn't believe. I just didn't know how I felt and it all seemed to stem from mixed religious energies I had encountered during my life. So when I placed this book down, I felt in my heart for the first time in my life that Jesus truly had walked this earth, and that He did indeed exist 2000 years earlier. At that point I became fascinated with the Holy Land and the fact that Jesus had lived there.

Later that year, in 1997, when I was spending some time in London, I decided to take a trip over to Israel. My New Zealand roommate, Page, thought it sounded like a fun trip and decided to join me. It was a couple of weeks before Xmas, so I thought a perfect time to visit, with Jesus' birthday around the corner.

The whole trip to Israel felt kind of surreal. One of my favorite memories was visiting the "Church of the Nativity" in Bethlehem, which was built on top of the first church built in 326 AD, which was said to have been built on top of the "Manger" where Jesus was born. It was a fascinating experience. Another favorite memory was visiting the "Garden

Tomb" outside the old city of Jerusalem. We also trekked to the Masada (an ancient mountaintop fortress) in the wee hours of the morning. From this high plateau, we overlooked the Dead Sea and watched the sun spread its new morning glory across the vast plains below us. We floated in the Dead Sea which was quite the experience in itself, then immediately following we crossed the street and washed the salt off in a beautiful, fresh, clear waterfall.

Page and I were staying at a small hotel outside the gates of the old city of Jerusalem. After a long day of sightseeing in this historical land, we were resting on a seat in the lobby chatting and laughing with a bright-eyed, redheaded lady who worked behind the desk. She was asking about our day when a feeling within urged me to tell her how I had felt in the old city that day. I told her, "I thought I would feel a presence of Jesus here in the old city, but I didn't. All I felt was mixed energies that didn't feel all that good." Instantly her bright eyes became even brighter, as she said, "Oh, you would like this other place outside the old city." She quickly added, "It is called *The Garden Tomb* and is owned and operated by a Ministry from England. They purchased the property in the 1890's."

The next day, Page and I visited The Garden Tomb. As we walked into the grounds a calming feeling came over me. It was quite a different experience than visiting the churches in the old city. A tall gentleman instantly walked over to us. He had a gentle smile and a calming presence about him. He said he was a Minister and then offered to show us around. We followed him along a meandering path, through a gorgeous garden, full of blooming flowers. As we strolled across a small bridge the Minister said, "I am going to point to the place where our Ministry believes Jesus was placed upon the cross. Also, I will take you to the cave where he was said to have been laid to rest. But I want you to keep in mind that this is what we have come to learn and believe. I suggest you trust what you feel within your own heart to be the truth."

If I could describe the way I was feeling in that moment as we passed over the small bridge, I would say it was as though I was smiling from the inside out. I looked around and felt complete serenity and comfort. I guess if anyone had ever asked me to describe what I would view in my mind as the beginning of time in the Garden of Eden, my surroundings certainly resembled the impression that I would share.

As we followed the meandering path the Minister pointed to some mustard plants. I instantly recalled Jesus' words from the bible about the mustard seeds. "If you have faith the size of a mustard seed, you will say to this mountain, 'Move from here to there,' and it will move; and nothing will be impossible to you." How appropriate I thought as I smiled to myself.

As we turned a corner, the Minister then pointed out to a cliff-face in the distance. He said, "The top of that cliff is where it has been said that Jesus was placed upon the cross." I stood very still for a moment while gazing up at the cliff-face. Then somewhere in my heart I felt that this may very well bear some truth or some significance to that period in time. It is hard to explain, but the feelings were strong and just felt right. I don't know if I had felt intuition quite this strong for some time. It seemed as though I was meant to be here and this was something I was supposed to witness.

Granted this place might have resembled the Garden of Eden, but more than that, there was definitely something unique and oddly humbling about this special garden. It was as though nothing demanded appreciation, not the Minister, not the flowers—it was as though "unconditional energy" rampaged through every crevice and crack of this entire garden. I don't know what it was, but something within just felt sort of...well, right.

We turned a corner back toward the entrance and to the right of us on a lower level was a cave. We walked down the steps and then entered the cave. The Minister turned to us and said, "This is the cave where it has been said that Jesus' body was laid to rest." The feeling I received within the cave was probably not quite the same feeling I had received at the cliff-face. If there was any part of this experience that didn't feel in line with the rest, this was probably it. Though, since my visit, I have heard countless remarks, stories, and conclusions leading to the understanding by many followers that this cave/garden tomb is in fact the resting place of Christ 2000 years earlier. So, maybe the whole experience was just taking its toll. I do remember feeling quite emotional that afternoon due to the unexpected energy that seemed to surge through me during this unique yet delightful adventure.

We headed back to the entrance where we found a small gift shop. I quickly came across these unusual bookmarks which had mustard seeds embedded on the front, next to Jesus' popular quote that had sprung to my mind earlier. Apparently the mustard seeds were taken from the mustard plants I had seen in the garden here. As I grabbed one for Mum and one for myself, I smiled in appreciation at this interesting day that had unfolded. However, I was soon to find out that this adventure wasn't quite over. Not for today anyway.

I looked up to see the Minister entering the gift shop. He walked over to where we were standing and asked if we had visited the Sea of Galilee. We hadn't. So he asked if we would be interested in seeing it that afternoon. Without any hesitation we accepted his kind offer. He went on to say that he would have his gardener get the car ready and asked us to meet him out front in 15 minutes.

On the way to Galilee, we shared stories with the gardener. He was a shy young man in his early 20's. We praised him for his beautiful work at the gardens where we had just visited. He smiled and humbly thanked us for our appreciation. It appeared that everything about that place revolved around a humbling energy. As I sat in the car enjoying this fascinating ride to Galilee I couldn't help but wonder if this humbling, quiet, and calming energy that surrounded the gardens and the people could possibly be an ongoing influence of Jesus' energy and teachings.

When we arrived at Galilee, I guess I expected something magical to happen. Maybe people walking on water or something like that. I don't know. Gusts of wind were picking up the swell of the water just like it does on any other large body of water. It reminded me of Lake Michigan in Chicago. It looked like the sea, and moved like the sea, but instead was just a very large lake. However alike they may be, the two are definitely incomparable in size. The gardener took us inside a nearby church, called "The Church of the Heptapegon," also known as "The Church of the Multiplication of loaves and fish." He took us to the front of the church where he showed us the "Byzantine Mosaic of Loaves and Fish," which were tiles depicting the story of Jesus feeding the people fish and bread.

Driving home in the car that afternoon, and looking back on the day, it all seemed so surreal. I remember feeling a closeness to Jesus that I had never felt before. And I knew in my heart that this would be a day that I would never forget.

For many years I was uncertain about Jesus and the probability of His existence and guidance. Yet today, due to my experience in Israel that year, and to a number of other unfolding experiences since that time, I feel blessed to have found the faith in His presence and guidance. I feel in my heart that He offered the Course to us to find our way home as He did. But...at the end of the day it really doesn't matter how or why we received A Course in Miracles. All that matters is that it is here now. And for some reason I felt a desire to share some of my journey that helped stage my faith and participation in Jesus' guidance which He offers in the Course.

Chapter 2

A Dream You Say?

THE JOURNEY BEGINS

I recently finished reading "The Disappearance of the Universe," by Gary Renard. Gary's book offers much clarity in areas where the Course can be quite difficult to understand. It has brought the light to truth in offering me an understanding of the *whole* on a brand new playing field. This playing field, which relates directly to the Course, I call "Playing Field Two" (PF2). As I look back at Laws of the Universe, including Law of Attraction, that I studied and followed this past decade, I find myself referring back to this as "Playing Field One" (PF1).

The difference between the playing fields is not so obvious. However, I will work at explaining the differences here to benefit anyone who might be journeying along a similar path as me (having partaken in PF1 in previous years). In PF1, we have the steering wheel and work at shifting and molding the clay, as we knowingly choose, to form manifestations. Our goal is to manifest all that we desire and be in control of all outcomes. In PF2, we no longer have the steering wheel. We move forward in complete guidance from the Source of Higher Knowing. We must hand the wheel over if we are to have faith on our journey home. And we must know that Holy Spirit is our Inner Voice (Voice for God), as well as the Source of Higher Knowing, and will guide us as necessary on the path that leads us to peace, freedom, and love—thence God. In PF2, an understanding that all our surroundings are part of an illusionary experience, or in other words a dream-state, is realized. We understand the egoic behavior that requires dissipation, and our goal is to release all that keeps us in wrong mind, remember the Truth which exists in our Right Mind, and return home.

As I sit here today in my townhome in Redondo Beach, I ponder the new idea that this, all around me, is an illusion. I look around at my home and take a moment for the thought to sink in. Hmm, if this is an illusion, then how can it be home? Home is where I am heading. It actually took me weeks to fathom the possibility that this might be an illusionary dream-state and get it somewhere in my head where it could sit for a while. I went to the beach many times and even shed a tear as I looked out to sea. And as I sat on the sands of Manhattan Beach I worked at coming to terms with the possibility that this was all somehow an illusion—a plain, simple, inconsequential illusion.

I was sad that this world around me (the world I thought I could create with as I wish) was all of a sudden a puff of nothing—a dream that would somehow disappear as soon as I came to remember who I am. After receiving clarity on this subject in the past weeks I have come to see that the possibility of the dream-state is something that I have no choice but to come to terms with. What I have been re-reading in the Course after all these years is finally making a lot of sense.

As I search my past studies regarding the Magnetic Laws of the Universe and the belief that everything is made up of energy, I find that this assists me in shedding some light on the "illusionary" concept I have come to understand so far within the Course. When we view everything as energy then wouldn't the idea that energy "is everywhere and through everything" offer insight that energy is the make-up of the dream—the illusion? Therefore, energy can be molded and shifted and can even disappear, offering further insight that what we see around us is in actual fact illusionary.

As the Course states in the preface, **"Nothing real can be threatened, Nothing unreal exists, herein lies the peace of God."** So, Truth cannot be threatened. Truth is ongoing...eternal. And nothing else exists; we merely think it does, based on assumptions which surface from our wrong mind. As I read this, I understand it, yet still find it difficult to fathom the reality behind the idea that nothing unreal exists. So another insight I find helpful is when I look at yesterday and ask myself how yesterday appears to me now? Yesterday appears as a dream really. I can't touch anything that I see in it. It is gone, like a puff of nothing, only memories in my mind. And then, on the other hand, I pretend I go forward in time, maybe one hundred years, and ask myself how would this existence look? I see that almost all of us wouldn't be here. To plop ourselves into this experience in one hundred years time, where we wouldn't know anybody or anything, then looking back on it, wouldn't it appear like a dream?

A MEANINGLESS WORLD

At the end of the day, I am coming to believe there is truth to this "dream-state" suggestion and that this around me—this now all of a sudden strange world around me—is one big fat dream. So, if I do want to wake up from this dream and return to where that pure loving energy resides (somewhere called home) then I guess I need to move forward with completing the lessons in ACIM.

The 365 lessons, one for each day of the year, are split into two parts. Part One and Part Two. As I sit here, I feel inspired to share my journey through these lessons with you. However, with 365 lessons, it would be difficult to share my entire journey. So, the lessons that do stand out to me and have a strong impact, I will share with you. I began the lessons a couple of weeks ago and am now at lesson 14. This lesson is having quite an impact on me and I feel the desire to share it. However, first, I do want to go back briefly to lesson 1, and offer some insight into the beginning of this journey.

Lesson 1. Nothing I see in this room [on this street, from this window, in this place] means anything. [WB, pg 3] It makes sense that if this is a dream, and is not the reality I once gave it, then I must begin to view objects around me differently. It does feel odd to view things around me as though they don't truly exist and as though they have no meaning. But if I am going to shift my focus and begin to see the Truth rather than the illusion then it makes sense that this is the path I must follow.

Over the past 2 weeks, the lessons seem to be "shifting" my previous thought process, or my perception, in relation to objects and matters of concern around me. The shift, though subtle, is becoming more noticeable as time goes by. However, it is not so easy to all of a sudden take a step back and come to terms with the fact that the chair I thought was a chair is no longer a chair. When I check in with my Higher Self about this, I get this feeling that tells me not to question my performance on the set tasks. However, this feeling tells me to trust that I am doing what is required within the guidelines of the Course, and to just know that all will unfold in the right, timely fashion.

From what I have come to understand about the Course, Jesus is guiding us on our path home, teaching us how to automatically forgive and peel back the egoic layers. Looking at the Workbook for students, it is obvious that it requires a dedicated amount of time and effort. However, it is stated that we need only complete the lessons one time.

What we are asking for in picking up the Course to begin with is the desire to find ultimate peace and harmony. Other students have told me that upon commencing the Workbook lessons the deepest, darkest parts of the wrong mind (ego) are prone to surface. This is so these fear-based egoic patterns can undergo a healing process. I guess as time moves forward, I will begin to understand what these students mean as aspects of my wrong mind surface for healing.

Many students have claimed that they stopped doing the lessons as the negative energy that surfaced had become too much to bare. They have also stated that when they stopped doing the lessons the unbearable darkness that was surfacing actually subsided. That makes sense. If we cease doing the lessons and put the Course down, then the desire to heal is no longer present, so the egoic layers that require healing are no longer in our face so to speak. To move toward enlightenment (waking up from the dream) wouldn't happen overnight, however, when the desire is great, I believe the healing can and will happen at a greater pace. Therefore, it makes sense that negative emotions will surface at a greater rate than before. If we no longer wish to tackle the negative emotions, and put the Course down and remove our focus from healing, the healing will cease to occur. Thus it makes sense that the negative emotions will rise as they did before, spasmodically, and not at the rapid, and possibly uncomfortable, pace.

I feel it is a good decision to put the Workbook down if the feeling arises within to do so. There is a time and place for all changes to occur. And I believe we know in our heart when the time is right for change. I know for myself I will trust my Inner Guidance as I go through the lessons, and whatever I feel guided toward I will follow.

MOVING FORWARD

As I read **lesson 14** today, **God did not create a meaningless world** [WB, pg 23], I pause to fathom the depth of that statement. I then read in the first paragraph... **What God did not create does not exist. And everything that does exist exists as He created it. The world you see has nothing to do with reality. It is of your own making, and it does not exist.** [WB, pg 23, 1.2]

In understanding that this whole universal experience is a dream, and an egoic dream at that, makes sense that it is not the creation of God as we have been led to believe. So, the fact that God did not create this seemingly existence and the Sonship merely fell asleep and dreamed of going into a body is shedding some light on the reason why "waking up" has been referred to in so much literature.

I suppose when I begin to see this world as meaningless I will begin to wake up. As I go about my day I have been reminding myself (as I do my lesson) that what I see is not real. What I see is a perception arising from the wrong mind.

To date I have come to understand from various teachings of the Course that the wrong mind is one wrong thought appearing as many. The one wrong thought being the initial thought of fear which seemingly divided and divided, thus creating a separation appearing as many forms. The Right Mind on the other hand is one whole. Nothing exists outside of the Right Mind. There is no awareness of separation. The awareness is Oneness.

TRUE PERCEPTION IS A CHOICE

I ponder the thought of perception and the important role it plays within this dream. Interestingly enough, I note that Holy Spirit is using our perception (once under complete management of the ego) to now assist in shifting our pattern of awareness toward our journey home. I turn to the Text to read a passage that offers some more clarity.

Perception selects, and makes the world you see. It literally picks it out as the mind directs. [Text, pg 456, 1.1]

I know this to be true. Over time, I have built my world upon what I desired, or not desired. What I have perceived as real is what *has* become my surroundings. Hearing the Voice that day that told me to stop visualizing is indication that my perception is ready to shift. Now I would choose not to choose, but to seek direction from the Voice within as I perceive my surroundings.

I had this list I put together a couple of years ago, where I listed the attributes of a special mate that I would like to meet and share my life with. This morning I had a feeling to rip up that list. So, I just took it off the back of the cupboard in the study (where it has been taped for a couple of years) then ripped it up and threw it away. It actually felt quite good. I wrote that list for the same reason that one would have a vision board—part of PF1 (Law of Attraction). So now it is in the hands of Holy Spirit, being PF2 (A Course in Miracles) and I will be guided to where Holy Spirit leads me. I wonder who Holy Spirit will choose for me? Or, I wonder if Holy Spirit will choose anyone at all? Maybe I will spend some more years on my own. It is all okay by me. The faith I feel to let it go and have Holy Spirit (the Voice within) decide for me feels good today.

Perception is a choice and not a fact. But on this choice depends far more than you may realize as yet. [Text, pg 456, 1.7]

As I look around me, I see that judgment is what arises from perception. And to look around and cease that judgment is what creates a shift in perception. Hmm, how do we know what we have always perceived to be "the truth" at the end of the day?

If we can open our minds and explore the possibility that past perception might not have been "true" perception, then we can open our hearts for whatever the Truth may be to pour in. But while we have the steering wheel and believe we know best, then we can't possibly be open to any other probability.

I muse over this shift in perception that the Workbook obviously is offering. This shift from thinking I understand everything around me to the realization that I really don't know much at all—which will enforce a new belief in everything that I perceive. I basically have no choice if I wish to move forward here. I must surrender all knowledge and all past learning and say, "Show me the way. Show me the Truth." Therefore, "Please correct my perception."

WELCOMING A SHIFT IN PERCEPTION

Today I have reached **lesson 24** in the Workbook. I pause to read my lesson. **I do not perceive my own best interests.** [WB, pg 36] I read on to paragraph 2. **If you realized that you do not perceive your own best interests, you could be taught what they are. But in the presence of your conviction that you do know what they are, you cannot learn. The idea for today is a step toward opening your mind so that learning can begin.**

I know I must begin to open my mind to the unknown. If I am to wake up from this dream, I must realize that all I *know* is this dream. And I must surrender the knowledge I once thought was real so I can begin to remember the Truth.

I am willing. Now I know where the truth lies. My heart tells me that truth resides within the Course. I am willing to forget all the knowledge that brought me to this point today. I am ready to live in the world but not of the world. As I look back, I realize that I have been controlling the outcome of my world. ACIM teaches me to release the control. I feel I am ready to hand over the steering wheel and have faith that the Voice within knows better than me.

ABOVE ALL ELSE I WANT TO SEE

Lesson 27. Above all else I want to see. [WB, pg 42] As I complete today's lesson I consider how strong my desire is to see the Truth. I read on to paragraph 4. **The real question is how often will you remember? How much do you want today's idea to be true? Answer one of these questions and you have answered the other.**

I believe I want to see the Truth. But am I remembering each day to look to the Truth? If I am forgetting on a daily basis to look to the Truth instead of judging, controlling etc., then I must not be wanting to "see" the Truth quite as bad as I think. A part of me feels like I do want to "see" the Truth. But I guess another part of me is very stuck in this dream.

I can tell that I will have to work at becoming more *aware* of exiting this dream. And I will have to become more *aware* of what the ego places in front of me to trip me up.

REMEMBERING THE TRUTH

Days are moving by and I feel tested every single day with what I perceive to be of value. Today's lesson is especially poignant as it is encouraging me to look around and decipher my values. **Lesson 32. I have invented the world I see.** [WB, pg 49] I read in the first paragraph...**While you want it you will see it; when you no longer want it, it will not be there for you to see.** [WB, pg 49, 1.5]

I have to realize the more value I place on material items around me the more value I offer to the dream. Is that my wish? To offer value to this dream? Because I can see now that that is what will keep me stuck. I have to be conscious of the value I place on my surroundings. What I see around me right now is not Truth. Do I believe that yet? I guess I must ask myself that question. I have to ask myself if I am ready to devalue what I see and have known all my life. I think I am. I believe what I am learning within the Course. But am I truly ready?

GOD GOES WITH ME EVERYWHERE I GO

It is a warm September day in Redondo Beach. I went for a walk this morning along the beach. I watched dolphins playing in the surf. Almost every time I walk the beach here I see dolphins. I love to watch them. It is as though they offer a message of freedom. These days, as I walk the beach, I revise my lesson. Today's lesson is **41. God goes with me everywhere I go.** [WB, pg 63] I do feel that when I wake up from this dream I will see that I never truly left God. I just thought I left Him. Or, I thought He left me is probably more to the truth. I pause to consider the dolphins...and then my lesson. If God goes everywhere with me then does He go everywhere with everyone and everything, including the dolphins? This feeling within tells me that God *resides* everywhere at all times. The only reason we don't see Him is because we have placed these illusionary figures where God exists. But God doesn't leave. The figures are illusionary, so they only appear to take up that space.

Now I am back at home, sitting on my balcony. It is so peaceful here. I have lived here for 5 years. However, I am beginning to feel a pull to go somewhere else. I don't know where yet. I think I could see myself living in Hawaii. Ever since the first time I visited Hawaii 15 years ago I felt that I could live there. I actually have a trip booked for this November to Oahu. I can't wait!

I pause to consider the continual presence of God in my life if I were to move to Hawaii. Granted many say that Hawaii is a spiritual land. However, it was here, in sunny California, where I first witnessed the presence of God in my life. I will share that story with you a little later. That was quite an eye opening day for me.

As I relax on my balcony a gentle reminder shifts my focus to the Workbook. I pick it up and turn to my lesson. I re-read the page from my lesson. The following sentences get my attention. **You can never be deprived of your perfect holiness because its Source goes with you wherever you go.** [WB, pg 63, 4.1] and then, **Nothing can destroy your peace of mind because God goes with you wherever you go.** [WB, pg 63, 4.4] I realize that I must remind myself continually that God is *always* with me. I wish I knew and felt one hundred percent in my heart that He was. How reassuring would that be? To know that always, and in all ways, God is with me. It would feel magnificent to know that God is walking with little ole me. That is how it feels. Me...just simple little ole me. Why would God want to walk with me of all people? Couldn't He get some more exciting moments from watching someone else live their life? Like the Queen? Wouldn't He prefer to walk with the Queen? A feeling comes over me that tells me I must work at realizing my Truth. It tells me I must learn to forgive the mistakes I have made in idolizing others and in seeing them as worthier than me. Now I must begin to fathom the truth of who I am...and the truth of who we all are. So I must come to the understanding that everyone and everything in this world is appearing as an illusionary fragment of the Whole. And that each one of us is in fact the holy Son of God. Then I can fathom the truth of God's presence. After all, from my understanding of reading the Course, the Sonship is an extension of God. But, then...I still get stuck in believing the fact that I am the *holy Son of God.*

I believe in the Course. I do. But do I for one second believe that I am the holy Son of God? Ha. The thought is actually quite hilarious. The thought of me standing up and saying I am the holy Son! Now, I can see someone like the Queen—this person we have been taught to idolize—standing up to say she is in fact the holy Son of God! The simple thought that we are *all* One as the holy Son of God (which makes us all equal) just seems so ludicrous and so opposing to everything that society has taught us. I guess looking at the feelings I am getting right now, and how separate I feel from my Truth, I had better quiet my mind and take a look at my lesson again.

21

Chapter 3

Hearing the Call for Love

THE TWO VOICES

There are two voices that reach for our attention throughout the day. They are the Voice of Love and the voice of fear. First of all, let me explain what I mean by voices. When I say, "Hear a voice," I don't mean a loud booming voice from the sky. It's not an audible voice outside of us. It is more like a feeling or sometimes even words from within that include a "push" or a "desire" in a certain direction.

When we ask ourselves a question we often hear two choices. The voice of fear most often dominates the Voice of Love. This is because we have chosen for a long time to pay more attention to the voice of fear. The voice of fear always lets us know that we need to *hang* on to something. It signals a *need* for things outside of us which might include material items and often individuals. Let's say for example, I am questioning a relationship that I have been involved in for a number of years. I ask myself whether or not to stay in this relationship. I might receive a feeling that says, "How could you possibly be alone if this relationship were to end?" Or, "How can you possibly be without this person after having them in your life for so long? These feelings are feelings of fear delivered from the voice of fear. Whenever we feel a *need* for something outside of ourselves (that struggling, trying feeling that we need to make something work) we are coming from *lack* which is what the voice of fear feeds us.

The Voice of Love lets us know that we can relax and let go of what is bothering us, and the outcome is sure to be good. It will gently guide us to stay in a relationship, or it will gently guide us away from a relationship. The Voice of Love *gently* guides us away from situations or people that are no longer required on our path, and it gently guides us toward situations and people who will play a significant role in our path. It doesn't mean that a person will be good or bad for us. The question to always ask is, "Is this person or situation right for me?" The Voice of Love will always answer gently and lovingly. The voice of fear will always answer out of need, struggle, and lack.

When you chose to leave Him He gave you a Voice to speak for Him because He could no longer share His knowledge with you without hindrance. [Text pg 76, 5.6]

To connect with and hear the Voice of Love (Voice for God) we must be patient. Many of us have listened to the voice of fear throughout much of our lifetime. So to now ignore that voice that we are accustomed to hearing is not so easy.

As time goes by it does get easier to catch the voice of fear, or in other words, the ego. Love gently pulls back the suffocating layers the ego embodies. As we come to understand the different voices we can ignore the ego and choose Love instead. For, as we continue to choose Love, the ego is peeled away yet again, and the Voice of Love shines through. Soon we distinguish the subtle differences and the Voice of Love gently and peacefully guides us home.

When the ego was made, God placed in the mind the Call to joy. This Call is so strong that the ego always dissolves at Its sound. That is why you must choose to hear one of two voices within you. One you made yourself, and that one is not of God. But the other is given you by God, Who asks you only to listen to it. [Text, pg 75, 3.2]

The Call to joy comes from the Voice of Love, which is the Voice for God—also known as the Holy Spirit. In every moment, we have freedom of choice. We can choose to listen to the Call to joy (Voice of Love) and be guided home to joy. Or, we can choose to listen to the ego (voice of fear) and stay stuck in the dream. To date, I have referred to the Voice of Love in various ways. For example: my Inner Voice, my Higher Self, my Inner Guidance, or my Soul. However, due to the Course's teachings, I am finding myself referring more to this Voice today as the Holy Spirit.

The Holy Spirit is in you in a very literal sense. His is the Voice that calls you back to where you were before and will be again. It is possible even in this world to hear only that Voice and no other. [Text, pg 75, 3.7]

I turn to my lesson. **Lesson 49. God's Voice speaks to me all through the day.** [WB, pg 78] I continue on to the first paragraph. **It is quite possible to listen to God's Voice all through the day without interrupting your regular activities in any way. The part of your mind in which truth abides is in constant communication with God, whether you are aware of it or not. It is the other part of your mind that functions in the world and obeys the world's laws. It is this part that is constantly distracted, disorganized and highly uncertain.** I recall a time when I was tested between the two voices. This day I was guided to Barnes & Noble where I picked up Gary

Renard's book, "The Disappearance of the Universe." When I picked up this book for the first time I felt a fear gush through my body and an impulse to place the book back upon the shelf. As I had studied the two voices previously, I knew that it was my ego, or in other words, fear, that was urging me to put the book down. However, I knew the Voice that had led me to Barnes and Noble that day was indeed the Voice of Love. I bought the book, took it home, yet continued having fearful feelings in regards to reading the book. I recall picking the book up to read the next day and this voice telling me immediately to put it back down. It was strong. My ego was unhappy for at least the first two weeks of me reading "The Disappearance of the Universe." I picked it up and put it down on several occasions. However, after the second week I settled into the read, and at that point couldn't put it down.

By the time I finished "The Disappearance of the Universe" I had become hooked on the Course. Gary and his teachers, Arten and Pursah, have since become one of my greatest mentors of ACIM. Another mentor who helped to clarify the message of ACIM is Ken Wapnick. Due to Gary Renard and Ken Wapnick's material, ACIM has quickly become one hundred percent clearer and much more interesting to me.

Some other wonderful Course teachers who have positively influenced my journey are Dr. Jerry Jampolsky, Beverly Hutchinson McNeff, Dr. Lee Jampolsky, and Judith Skutch Whitson. I feel blessed to have been inspired by each of these teachers and to listen to their words of wisdom in sharing the Course.

FORGIVENESS IS MY FUNCTION

There are multiple review lessons in the Course. The lessons I have been reviewing in the recent weeks are lessons 51-60. I like reviewing the lessons. This newfound knowledge is taking some time to sink in so I could certainly do with a reminder.

When someone asks me to give a definition of the Course to them, I tell them it is a book about forgiveness. It is about forgiving everything we have made real within the dream. It is forgiving all that we thought our brother did to us plus forgiving ourselves for anything we appeared to have done to our brother. I understand that this sounds like quite the task. Believe me I am still getting a handle on the fact that everything around me isn't real. It is mind-blowing to suddenly push into my awareness a whole new idea that everything I see, everything I hear, and everything I touch, so in other words, virtually everything I know to date…is an illusion.

I have read about forgiveness at length in the Text, and have some insight; however, I am yet to complete any forgiveness lessons in my life. I am unsure of how to implement them at this stage. Maybe times are going to change, as **lesson 62,** my lesson for today, is the first lesson I have come across so far in the Workbook that highlights forgiveness. I take a moment to read my lesson. **Forgiveness is my function as the light of the world.** [WB, pg 104] I read on to paragraph 3. **Remember that in every attack you call upon your own weakness, while each time you forgive you call upon the strength of Christ in you. Do you not then begin to understand what forgiveness will do for you? It will remove all sense of weakness, strain and fatigue from your mind. It will take away all fear and guilt and pain. It will restore the invulnerability and power God gave His Son to your awareness.** I guess this is saying that in my attack toward my brother I am calling on the darkness. In other words I am calling on the ego. Yet, as I relinquish my defenses, and instead see the truth (forgiveness) I enable myself to see the Light in my brother and also in myself.

I know in my heart I want to see the Light. I want to free my brother and free myself. I only pray that I will be given the ability and wisdom that enables me to always forgive. I understand what it is saying, but how do I truly forgive in a way that makes sense to me? It seems that today's lesson is offering me a small shift toward understanding forgiveness. I want the shift. I guess I am being hard on myself, and I need to be patient. I have to have faith that as I do these lessons, no matter how small a difference each one seems to make, that as time moves forward I will learn to forgive in line with the teachings of the Course.

LOVE CREATED ME LIKE ITSELF

It is another perfect, sunny day in California. I love summer. I often dream of living an endless summer between Australia, Hawaii, and California. We are in mid October, and it is like a glorious summer's day! I just got back from my morning walk along the beach. I saw heaps of dolphins. Actually, it is very surprising if I don't see at least one dolphin on my morning walk. The water is quite motionless in the mornings, making it easy to spot them. They swim along the shoreline, right where the waves begin to pick up some swell. On occasion, I have seen dolphin's swim right by a surfer, within only a couple of yards, while perched on their board waiting for that next wave.

Now I am back at home sitting on my balcony, enjoying the morning sunshine while eating a bowl of cereal. I turn to my lesson for the day. **Lesson 67. Love created me like Itself.** [WB, pg 113] I read in the second paragraph. **We will begin by repeating the truth about you, and then spend a few minutes adding some relevant thoughts, such as:**
Holiness created me holy.
Kindness created me kind.
Helpfulness created me helpful.
Perfection created me perfect.

Any attribute which is in accord with God as He defines Himself is appropriate for use. We are trying today to undo your definition of God and replace it with His Own. We are also trying to emphasize that you are part of His definition of Himself. [WB, pg 113, 2.2]

I stop to consider the thought that God is holy, kind, helpful, and perfect. So I look at myself (created in His image) and see that I must also be created as holy, kind, helpful, and perfect. Hmm, then how come the thought fills my head instantly that I am not all these things? Is that my wrong mind beckoning me to remain in numbness? To believe I am not worthy of Love? To believe I am not worthy to *be* Love? It is sad that I foster these thoughts of myself, and see myself as imperfection. I feel in my heart that I just *might* be an essence of God's Being and am formed from His Loving existence. But, there is something else inside of me that says, "You are not all that. There is someone out there who is better than you! How can you think that you are close to perfect?" This voice is bigger. This voice of the wrong mind, of the ego, is large. I wish the Voice of Love was larger. So large that I could see my true Identity soar across the sky. I hate the fact that this wrong voice has gotten a hold of my mind. I want to remember who I am! I want to replace these ill thoughts with loving thoughts about myself. It can't be soon enough!

How can I move forward every day with this new knowledge that I am suffering a type of amnesia? That I truly don't even know myself? It is as though someone has cast a spell on me, taken my Identity, stricken me with insanity, and is laughing about all of it. I feel trapped in a body that I don't even know anymore. Is it truly a dream-state? A body that wasn't there, that isn't there now, and will have no recollection when I wake up? How can I continue with life the way it was?

I have a million questions, and all of a sudden there is nobody to answer them for me. Not in the way that I need to hear them anyway! *I need to hear the truth from the Truth!* I need to scream it from the rooftop so the Truth knows I am ready to hear it. Holy Spirit is the Truth. So I want to know Holy Spirit, and I want to know and connect more fully with Jesus. I need to identify with these figures, for they bear the Truth! I feel for the first time in my life that I have no-one to turn to, and no-one to pose a question to—not *out there* anyway. I have to turn within in each step, not just sometimes like before in PF1, but all the time. I have to face the Truth within if I want to recall who I am. Nobody else can show me the essence of *me*. Now I realize more than ever that I must look to Holy Spirit for every single answer. I knew before, in PF1, how important it was to listen *within*. But I still figured that we as humans were important, that we were very real, and that I could turn to another for a mathematical answer that mattered! Now I have to see that we were only sleepwalking and thinking that everything we see is our reality. That 1 + 1 really equals 2! That reminds me of one of Ken Wapnick's CD's, called "When 2 + 2 = 5." If it is illusionary does it really matter if 1 + 1 = 2? Is that really worth giving the time of day to when I don't even *know* who I am?

If I am holiness, if I am perfection, then where did I get off the "knowing" train? When did I stop believing in who I am? Why did I stop believing in who I am? How can I even begin to remember who I am? I guess I have to forgive everything that I thought I was. And realize that there is nobody out there to blame. I have to forgive everything. And then if I want to remember who I truly am, I guess I have to make way for the Truth to enter. I have to remove all prior knowledge now. I have to forgive everything that I thought happened to me. I have to forgive everyone that judged me. And seeing all judgment starts with self, I have to forgive myself for ever judging myself! I have to forgive everything I thought I knew. I even have multiplication tables to forgive! I guess I better start *forgiving.*

OUT WITH THE OLD—IN WITH THE NEW

This past week I have been giving a lot of consideration toward removing old thought patterns about myself and those around me. I want to have good thoughts and feelings. But I know that it isn't enough to just want that. I must do the work. And the work is forgiveness. I have spent time thinking about forgiveness and the intricate web of undoing this wrong mind, and I have come to the realization that this "remembering," or in other words, this "waking up," is truly a miracle in itself. Each and every forgiveness of the falseness will bring us one step closer to the Truth, and I am learning that each small step is truly a miracle! I turn to **lesson 77** [WB, pg 137] **I am entitled to miracles.** I read paragraph 3. **Today we will claim the miracles which are your right, since they belong to you. You have been promised full release from the world you made. You have been assured that the Kingdom of God is within you, and can never be lost. We ask no more than what belongs to us in truth.**

I do feel that miracles are my natural right. I also feel that miracles will come about as I make this decision to stay with the Course. I feel in my heart that if I don't make that decision, and if I don't take this seriously, then miracles can't possibly be mine. I must make that decision. I must decide to wake-up. If I choose the dream, then I choose to stay asleep. Miracles can't ignite in the faces of those sleeping. I realize more than ever how important it is that I take this journey. So if miracles are my right, and if I do the work, they will offer me my memory back. I can't even begin to fathom the joy in that. To remember who I am seems impossible at this point. But it says right there in today's lesson, that I have been *promised* full release from the world I made. I have to have faith. But I feel myself getting tense; I feel the anxiety of doing the work. I have to relax and know that all will unfold perfectly. I have to trust. I can do this.

MIRACLES ARE SEEN IN LIGHT

As I wake up this morning I am excited about my trip to Hawaii next month. With no immediate family to spend Thanksgiving with here in the States, I couldn't think of a better place than Hawaii to spend some time in reflecting on some good ole customary "thanks." I love Hawaii. It is my favorite place in this dream! Warm evenings, clear waters, great energy, and best of all the lush, green, tropical landscape! The first time I set foot in Hawaii, back in 1993, on the island of Oahu, I called home and told Mum and Dad how much I loved it. Mum told me when she felt my excitement for Hawaii she thought I would never come home. There was a wonderful feeling I had about this beautiful land. I had not felt like that about anywhere else in all my travels. And I had previously travelled across 4 continents. I felt back then, and still feel today in my heart, that one day I will live in this paradise called Hawaii. And in just 29 days I will be there once again!

So far, I have been enjoying my lessons. I haven't noticed a lot of changes in my life at this point by doing them. I am just plodding along and completing them to the best of my ability. Sometimes I feel as though I don't give one hundred percent effort, so I end up doing the same lesson again the next day. I just trust the guidance I receive as to whether I need to spend more time on that lesson or not. I don't know if or when I am meant to notice a lot of changes from doing these lessons. The only change I have noticed recently is that each day I am feeling a little more accepting that this world around me is a dream. To date that has been the hardest part of completing the lessons for me...coming to terms with the fact that I am actually trapped in an ongoing dream.

I have just finished reviewing the lessons 81-90. It sure does help to reinforce the lesson's message when I do a review on it. I can also see how helpful it will be to revisit the lessons again (after completing all of them) to remind myself of the

31

important message that is being delivered in each one of them. Today I turn to **lesson 91. Miracles are seen in light.** [WB, pg 156] I read on to paragraph 2. **To you, then light is crucial. While you remain in darkness, the miracle remains unseen.** When I think of the ego and how it gets a hold sometimes is when I can tell that I am on my own. Higher Knowing can't come through when I am fearful and in wrong mind. When I am in wrong mind I am disconnected and can't hear what Holy Spirit is trying to signal through to me. So this makes sense to me that light is crucial, for miracles can only be seen in light and not in darkness. If I allow darkness to take a hold then I am giving up on miracles in that moment. I have to remember this and work at connecting to my Truth as much as I can.

COMING TOGETHER WITH COURSE STUDENTS

Today I received a CD in the mail from the "Miracle Distribution Center" in Anaheim. The CD is a taping of the evening's interactions at a recent study group I attended at the Miracle Distribution Center. I have attended this study group on a few occasions and truly enjoyed learning from Beverly Hutchinson McNeff. If you ever have the opportunity to visit her study group I highly recommend it. It is definitely a treat for any Course student.

This particular evening, we discussed "Grandeur versus Grandiosity." Today, I have been listening to the CD I received in the mail. It has reinforced a very important message which we discussed that evening. There was a section from the Text that Beverly asked me to read aloud to the group. This is what I read: **Grandeur is of God, and only of Him. Therefore it is in you. Whenever you become aware of it, however dimly, you abandon the ego automatically, because in the presence of the grandeur of God the meaningless of the ego becomes perfectly apparent. When this occurs, even though it does** not understand it, the ego believes that its "enemy" has struck, and attempts to offer gifts to induce you to return to its "protection." Self-inflation is the only offering it can make. The grandiosity of the ego is its alternative to the grandeur of God. Which will you choose? [Text, pg 177, VIII. Grandeur versus Grandiosity, 1.1]

The grandeur is of God, and the grandeur exists within me also. I must acknowledge this to be my truth; otherwise I will remain oblivious to the fact that I am the holy Son of God. It is becoming clearer how the ego seems to get into any nook and cranny in an effort to keep the dream alive. While I succumb to the ego's attempts at self-inflation, I will continue to slumber. I must work at being very aware of the ego's attempts to sway me with grandiosity. When this happens I need to be aware of my choice—grandeur or grandiosity. I must listen to my truth. *The grandeur is of God, and the grandeur exists in me also.*

JOINING AS ONE

I have been spending most of my waking time, hmm, well really my sleeping time, mulling over this new information. Sometimes, I feel I am getting a hold of it, and other times I feel like I might just remain asleep forever! One thing I know for sure is that I never doubt the information I am receiving. I feel deep in my heart that this is the truth. However, coming to terms with making this a part of my every day seems far from possible at this point.

I turn to my lesson for the day, **lesson 97.** [WB, pg 172] **I am spirit.** And read on to paragraph 2. **We state again the truth about your Self, the holy Son of God Who rests in you, whose mind has been restored to sanity. You are the spirit lovingly endowed with all your Father's Love and peace and joy. You are the spirit which completes Himself, and shares His**

function as Creator. He is with you always, as you are with Him.

I need to work on this each day. The fact that I am the holy Son of God is still mind blowing. I mean I can understand that Jesus is the holy Son of God. But me...the holy Son of God also? I learned in PF1 that I was spirit, and not this body. I learned that I was created in God's image. But I had no idea that I was *also* the holy Son of God! I guess I am beginning to come to terms with the fact that Jesus and I are "One." Also that everyone else who is on this journey, and in this dream, is also the holy Son of God—meaning we are "One." It makes me realize how much we have lost ourselves on this journey. We think that we are not worthy enough to be the holy Son of God!

If I wish to continue on this journey toward waking up, I had better get pretty good at understanding who I truly am. A feeling tells me to write it down, to make it sink in, and to relish in the fact that I am so much more than I ever thought I was. My Higher Self (Holy Spirit) wants me to know this in my heart, and savor it, and never lose it again. I feel that. Yet I know that it is going to take some work. Surprise, surprise, more work...but who said *A Course in Miracles* was going to be an easy walk? No wonder why it is called the *Workbook!* No getting off easy here. At the end of the day I have to really want this. I can see that now. I have to really want the *memory* back—the memory of my Truth.

WILL I ACCEPT MY PART?

I consider the thought of salvation. What is salvation to me? The Course is leading me down my path to salvation. I am being saved from my dream of illusionary sins. But how do I play my part in this? I repeat my lesson for the day, **lesson 98. I will accept my part in God's plan for salvation.** [WB, pg 174]

I ask myself, "What am I accepting?" Am I accepting something I can handle? Can I play my part?" It seems like Jesus could play this part, but what about me? Again, I am putting myself on that lower shelf, in believing I am not good enough to be the holy Son of God. I can see that if I don't begin to get my head around the fact that I *am* the holy Son of God then I simply cannot take this journey and play my role in salvation that I came forward to play. Isn't that what I want? Yes, I do. I want to play the role that will assist the Sonship as a whole to wake up.

Chapter 4

Inviting the Truth

FINDING THE STILLNESS AMONGST THE NOISE

The noise of the ego plays a part in my every day. Looking in from the outside, one would find me to be a happy soul. I mean I feel happy and I feel good most of the time. But, as time goes by, I am coming to understand the operation of the ego more and more. Each day I become increasingly aware of my hands on the steering wheel. And each day I release the wheel only to take it back again shortly thereafter. It is amazing how much the ego dominates our existence without us even realizing it. I am asleep more than I ever realized.

My thoughts drift to Hawaii, and the peace and serenity that fill my mind there. My trip is fast approaching. 12 sleeps to go! With good thoughts of Hawaii in my mind I turn to my lesson for the day, **lesson 106. Let me be still and listen to the truth.** [WB, pg 190] I read on to paragraph 1. **If you will lay aside the ego's voice, however loudly it may seem to call; if you will not accept its petty gifts that give you nothing that you really**

want; if you will listen with an open mind, that has not told you what salvation is; then you will hear the mighty Voice of truth, quiet in power, strong in stillness, and completely certain in Its messages.

The voice of fear sounds so reassuring at times. Like when I hear, "Robyn, it makes you feel good, you know that. Go this way, or do this thing." I follow that path, and then realize after the event that I didn't listen to the Voice of Love. The voice of fear was dominant, and I didn't even see it at the time! It is amazing just how much we like to control outcomes in our life, and we don't even know we are doing it. I never realized the ego played that much of a part in my everyday life. Those subtle thoughts and feelings of the ego—those times when *I think I know best.* Hmm, I really don't know best. Holy Spirit knows best. However, I find myself taking the wheel back again and again.

I wonder when I will get good at catching every aspect of the ego right off the bat. I hope it is sooner than later. As I have this thought, I get a feeling from within that tells me to spend some quiet time to assist in remembering who I truly am. Then as my memory returns I will be more *aware* of the false thoughts that enter my head. So that is what I will do for now. I will work at remembering my Truth.

I AM AS GOD CREATED ME

I feel that when I can truly apply today's lesson to every thought throughout every day is when I will feel free. **Lesson 110. I am as God created me.** [WB, pg 199] I read on to paragraph 1.2. **For this one thought would be enough to save you and the world, if you believed that it is true. Its truth would mean that you have made no changes in yourself that have reality, nor changed the universe so that what God created was replaced by fear and evil, misery and death. If**

you remain as God created you fear has no meaning, evil is not real, and misery and death do not exist.

If someone were to say to me, "Hey, you are as God created you"... I would believe them and say, "Oh, sure." But then if that were the truth, wouldn't I feel different as I walked about my day? Wouldn't I come from a loving place *all* the time if I truly believed I was blessed enough to be a creation of God? Wouldn't all fear be gone from my mind? Would I fear anything at all if I knew I was an essence of God's creation?

I still feel as though I am on my own. Why would I feel that way, but still believe that God created me? How can I feel different? How can I naturally *know* in each step that I am a creation of God? This gentle feeling that comes to me tells me to relax and in time I will remember my Truth. It seems this whole *remembering who I am* is the essence of this work—the light at the end of the tunnel. When I know who I am then maybe I can walk around with a different approach to life. A fearless approach. A more loving approach. A feeling tells me to spend quiet time with *new* thoughts about myself—like forgetting who I was, and working at remembering who I truly am. How can anyone tell me who I am? I guess no-one can. I have to make that decision that I truly *do* want to remember.

TIME TO FLY

I love to travel and write. So I have decided to make my trip to Hawaii a working holiday. Any excuse for a holiday! Seriously though, Hawaii is that type of place where you can really connect to your Truth and allow the Voice of Love to flow through. I have found in the past that some of my best writing has flowed through the energies of the aloha spirit.

I double check my packing. 2 dresses, 2 bikinis, 2 sarongs, 2 flip-flops, and a toothbrush. Ready! Just joking. I'm a female remember! Well, I'm not a big packer type really...I don't think. However, I have gotten pretty good at cramming enough beachwear in an overhead just because I am not a "checking in" type. If I can get away without checking in baggage, I will. I love to make the most of my time in Hawaii and get to the beach at the earliest opportunity, and later on this arvo (slang for "afternoon" in Oz) that's where I'll be!

LOOKING AT TRUTH

The flight to Honolulu went by very fast. It seemed as though we were in the air for about 2 hours as opposed to 5 hours. We took off, watched a movie, then I read for a bit, and the next thing we were making our descent for Honolulu! I am not sure why, but I do love to fly. So that helps time to pass by. Hmm, I suppose flying is a time where I get my "Robyn time." Time to relax, time to read, and time to stare into space, doing nothing and thinking about nothing. A time to get truly connected.

So here I am in fabulous Hawaii, where I have been thoroughly enjoying the aloha spirit! I am staying on the island of Oahu. This island has so much to offer from its rich turquoise waters, and defined mountain tops, to its lush, tropical landscapes and warm, balmy evenings. I can't stop smiling every time I spend time here on this island. I haven't put pen to paper for a couple of days. Some friends from the mainland are also visiting at this time. So I have been having some fun, just relaxing, swimming, sunning, and singing some karaoke with my friends!

Today is Thanksgiving Day. This day causes me to reflect on family, friends, and life. Why did I move to America more than a decade ago? Why was I okay leaving my family and friends in Sydney? As I lay on the beach looking out at the clear blue Hawaiian waters I recall the feeling that gently urged me to move to America. I remember that feeling that was unquestionable. I just knew in my heart I had to go to America. At the time I was on a quest for understanding myself. I knew there was a greater awareness within me, a greater awareness that guided me through gut feelings.

It was in Southern California, where I have spent the last 11 years, that I found a connection with this best friend—my Higher Self. The material provided to me that assisted me on this quest wasn't so readily available at the time in Australia. For this reason I believe my urge to spend time in California was undeniably an instinct, from my Higher Self, as a measure to get to know my Higher Self.

It is interesting to me how life changes so much and we never truly know where we are heading. However, I have come to understand that this other part of us, our Higher Self, now better known as Holy Spirit, knows everything about our present, past, and future. Why everything has happened. Why everything will happen. There is an ultimate destiny that Holy Spirit is guiding us toward. Everything we do or say, and everywhere we go, is taking us to this one place. If we get lost, are in despair, or feel confused, this is still part of the journey. We must know the dark before we can decide against it. In each moment, we face new choices. How can we rightfully choose a path when neither alternative is understood? Yet to make that choice, it is vital that we understand the subtle difference between the voice of fear and the Voice of Love.

CONNECTING WITH HOLY SPIRIT

The Holy Spirit is in your right mind, as He was in mine. The Bible says, "May the mind be in you that was also in Christ Jesus," and uses this as a blessing. It is the blessing of miracle-mindedness. It asks that you may think as I thought, joining with me in Christ thinking. [Text, pg 73, 3.3]

I would like to share with you how I came to understand and develop communication with my Inner Voice—Holy Spirit. For I believe good communication with Holy Spirit is vital if we wish to proceed along the path toward waking up.

To get better connected and to understand the guidance we receive from Holy Spirit, we must take quiet time and go within. When we are alone, feeling relaxed, and at peace, we are then able to better connect and receive guidance from Holy Spirit.

To strengthen our connection to Holy Spirit, I suggest spending some time in meditation. When I say meditation, I am not referring to lengthy intervals of in-depth meditation and/or humming. There is certainly nothing wrong with that, however, I am only referring to some general quiet time placed aside where there is zero interference from the outer world. The length of time does not matter, nor does the approach you might take. What *feels* good will be good, and will work. If you feel like humming, by all means, go ahead and hum. All that matters is that you are not being interrupted and the mind can become rested into a place where communication with Holy Spirit can naturally occur. If you have trouble relaxing, then paying attention to your breathing can assist in clearing that annoying mind chatter. Once your head is clear and you are feeling at peace and relaxed, then any impulses, gentle words, gut feelings, or general guidance can be felt/received from Holy Spirit.

Becoming familiar with our connection to Holy Spirit through meditation assists us in understanding how this connection feels while going about our daily life and interacting with others. We will also naturally become more aware each time a disconnection occurs within (fearful/negative feelings), and will quickly be able to identify the current wrong-minded thought that is causing the disconnection from Holy Spirit.

Holy Spirit is always ready to offer guidance when we are ready to receive it. We are ready to receive it when we give up control (when we let go of the trying, struggling, frustration, worry, or anger) for that is when we begin to relax and connect. Every time we connect consciously with Holy Spirit, our *awareness* of connection becomes strengthened. Having *faith* in the information that we are receiving also strengthens our connection with Holy Spirit.

Anytime we hear or feel guidance from Holy Spirit, it is a Call toward our awakening—a Call to know the Truth. This Call to our awakening is a Call to all. Not one individual will be left alone to wander the dark streets. We will each hear the Voice when we are ready to hear it.

As a man and also one of God's creations, my right thinking, which came from the Holy Spirit or the Universal Inspiration, taught me first and foremost that this Inspiration is for all. I could not have It myself without knowing this. The word "know" is proper in this context, because the Holy Spirit is so close to knowledge that He calls it forth; or better, allows it to come. I have spoken before of the higher or "true" perception, which is so near to truth that God Himself can flow across the little gap. Knowledge is always ready to flow everywhere, but it cannot oppose. Therefore you can obstruct it, although you can never lose it. [Text, pg 74, 4.6]

In this excerpt from the Course Jesus tells us that Holy Spirit offered Him Inspiration when He walked the earth, or in other words, when He was asleep within this dream. Holy Spirit guided Jesus toward the Light and toward waking up. And Holy Spirit will guide us in the same way.

Jesus is also telling us we can obstruct the flow of knowledge, although it is always there and always willing to flow to us. When we release control and relax, we connect with Holy Spirit and knowledge naturally enters our awareness.

GOD, BEING LOVE, IS ALSO HAPPINESS

Lessons 111-120 are review lessons. As I sit on my balcony, looking out over Diamond Head, I take in the beauty and then pause to do my review lesson, **lesson 117. God, being Love, is also happiness.** [WB, pg 210] I look all around, at the park, the zoo, and the ocean. I see pink flamingos in the distance and listen to the monkeys singing up a storm. They must have enjoyed the tropical downpour we had this morning. Either that or they are mimicking one of my rough attempts at karaoke last night!

The sky is now clearing and the sun spreads its light revealing the turquoise color in the ocean below. As I gaze at the beauty I recall what Ken Wapnick had told me at a recent seminar, "Enjoy the beauty and then smile, remembering in the back of your mind it is an illusion." I look at the beauty and smile as I recall Ken Wapnick's words and realize there is no need to give it any meaning. It just is what it is...a dream. Yet in this moment I do find it difficult to enjoy it without some sort of attachment to it.

As I look upon this beauty and repeat my lesson, **God, being Love, is also happiness,** a feeling comes over me, "*God is here...this feeling said, and I sensed He was all around.*" Then in the next instant I sensed God within and around everything. God exists within Diamond Head, the ocean, the zoo, the park, and even the animals. God is everywhere...and truly everywhere! As I gaze around I feel Love absolutely everywhere. I even feel Love within the table and chair on my balcony. It dawned on me that God could not "not exist" anywhere, for nothing was more powerful than the Love of God. God just simply is *everywhere.*

This moment takes me back in time (a few years ago) to an early summer morning in Hermosa Beach, California, where I was spending some quiet time alone in meditation. I had been questioning God. I wanted to know who He was. And I wanted to know where He was etc. As I sat in silent meditation I received an interesting vision and then this poem below:

A Loving Invitation

I feel an inner strength that I've never felt before;
It takes me to new heights and I see an open door.
I know not to push it, I feel that deep inside;
Allow it to just be and soon it'll open wide.
I see it open inch by inch as time passes by,
I stand and peek through and know soon I'll understand why.
Then one day I get a feeling, "Hey look at the door,"
It's open very wide now; I wonder when I'll explore.
I get another feeling and gently this is how it went...
"Do you want to go now? You are ready to advent."
I start to get excited as I float up from the ground,
I get a feeling in my back; it's wings I see I've found.
I can feel them start to flutter as I move on through the door;
This new world is so beautiful, and then there's even more...
A way to describe it would be like Alice's Wonderland;
Natural beauty boasting definition and clarity in each stand.
I think I'll be an angel with these new wings I have found,
But something said inside, "You're a butterfly that's abound."
I'm feeling very beautiful as I flutter through the air,
Then I said, "Okay, what's over here that wasn't over there?"
This feeling pulsed my body, though words cannot be found...
"God is here" this feeling said, and I sensed He was all around.
My blood a rush, I knew right then why this had to be;
I invited God into my world...and now He's invited me!

As I looked out over my balcony this morning, contemplating the thought of how I could enjoy this illusion, I believe that the line from my poem..."*'God is here', this feeling said, and I sensed He was all around,"* was given to me so I would remember what I had received in meditation back then and apply it to the beauty today.

My first instinct when I looked at the beauty this morning was almost one of guilt. How could I do the Course and then enjoy the beauty in this world also? My feelings tell me to see beyond the beauty to the *true* beauty underneath. This is where Love exists. This is where happiness exists. This is where God exists. God is truly everywhere. Nothing can remove the Love of God. God gently rests everywhere and within everything, awaiting our desire to awaken from this dream. Love always was there, is always there, and will always be there.

As I breathe in all the love within the ocean, park, and mountain I pause to do the second half of my lesson **[117]** for the day, **I seek but what belongs to me in truth.** [WB, pg 210, 2.1] As I breathe in the love I feel that I am breathing in my truth; the happiness, peace, abundance. It is all me. It is my birthright as the Son of God. I am this Truth that I breathe in. I am this Love that lies everywhere. God created *me* in His image, and He created *you* in His image.

4. You are the means for God; not separate, nor with a life apart from His. His life is manifest in you who are his Son. Each aspect of Himself is framed in holiness and perfect purity, in love celestial and so complete it wishes only that it may release all that it looks upon unto itself. [Text, pg 519]

5. Since you believe that you are separate, Heaven presents itself to you as separate, too. Not that it is in truth, but that the link that has been given you to join the truth may reach to you through what you understand. Father and Son and Holy Spirit are as One, as all your brothers join as one in truth. [Text, pg 519]

If I am to wake up from this dream—this illusion—then I must remember the truth. Yesterday is but a memory, it is like a dream. At the end of this lifetime, I will look back on it like I would a dream. Why not see it for what it really is today? For the only other alternative is to remain in the dream and awaken later. Why wake up later and not now? If I wake up now, then I can live the remainder of this life from my *Truth*. When I live from my Truth I rise above the pain and suffering. If I remain in the dream I welcome pain and suffering.

Today I received an email from a friend who has a timeshare on the island of Maui. He asked me if I would like to use his December week as he is unable to use it himself. So, I have been spending some time today looking into what it would entail for me to stay on Oahu longer and then go to Maui for a week. Unfortunately, it looks like I am unable to arrange the dates to stay for the period required. But I will look into it some more when I return to the mainland. I can see myself spending more time in Hawaii. I have been to Maui once before and really enjoyed it. Somehow I don't think I could visit any Hawaiian island and not enjoy it. So then I guess if I am meant to spend some more time with aloha energy then Holy Spirit will take me to Maui!

Chapter 5

Making the Choice to Detach

UNDERSTANDING DETACHMENT IN A SPIRITUAL LAND

Once I arrived back in California, some events unfolded which lined my dates up perfectly to enjoy a week in Maui. Woohoo! So here I am back in Hawaii, on the island of Maui. Mele Kalikimaka! It is the week before Xmas, and how fun it is to be here amongst the aloha Xmas energy.

As I look out over the colorful ocean of Ka'anapali, I think to myself if there is one place that tests my ability and the desire to stick with the Course and exit this dream, Hawaii has to be the place! Have I told you how much I love Hawaii?? I have decided I don't mind which island. I love them all!

I stop to consider what it is that allows me to enjoy this paradise and still move forward with the Course. I ponder the thought. All of a sudden I realize there is no attachment. I enjoy the colorful scenery, the bright energy of the people, and the spiritual essence of Ka'anapali, but now I am learning to release it at the same time! This feels good.

I guess it is the same with everything in life. We have to give up attachment. I never quite got it. I mean that saying of "giving up attachment." I used to think, "Well if I don't yearn for it then I'm not attached to it." I realize now as I look out over the ocean toward the beautiful island of Molokai...there is a fine line between attachment and detachment.

True detachment is being okay if I never hold this memory again. Knowing there is something more—something powerfully more satisfying. I say to myself, "Well this is quite satisfying to the palate, but you mean it gets better than this?" I hear this gentle voice say, "Oh Robyn, it gets so much better than this!" I smile to myself, knowing that I am never alone. Over time, as I have opened more and more for Holy Spirit to come through and speak to me, I feel like there is Love above me, mixed in me, next to me, in the next room, and down the corridor. Love is always ready to speak to me...whenever I am ready to listen.

Love never leaves me; however, I can choose to leave Love. I have absolute freedom wherever I go and whatever I do. I pause to repeat my lesson for the day, **lesson 132. I loose the world from all I thought it was.** [WB, pg 242] These days it is feeling less painful to give up the world as I have known it. When I became serious about the Course, I recall feeling very afraid and lost to know that this world was not all I thought it was. I couldn't quite grasp that everything I saw, everything I heard, and everything I touched was illusionary.

So, apparently, I fell asleep and now I am beginning to wake up from this dream where the ego dominantly played his role. I fell asleep and this is where the egoic wrong mind took over. Now as I awaken, my Identity returns to my awareness. Hmm, my Truth returns—my pure Loving State returns.

These lines in today's lesson offer a lot of clarity. **There is no world apart from what you wish and hearin lies your ultimate release. Change but your mind on what you want to see, and all the world must change accordingly.** [WB, pg 242, 5.1] I will take this thought with me today. "Change my mind and the world changes with me." That old saying, "It's all in your mind" I feel is a lot closer to the truth than many of us realize. As I ponder this thought my eyes rest on a white sail boat passing along the Ka'anapali coastline.

This feeling inside me says, "Change your mind Robyn—from your wrong mind to your Right Mind." Yes, that makes sense. The Right Mind is the awakened mind, and the wrong mind is the one that fell asleep. The wrong mind is filled with fear. The Right Mind is filled with Love.

Just then as I watch the sail boat drift off into the distance my thoughts wander to Jerry Jampolsky's book, "Love is letting go of fear." I love this book. It offers a simple yet powerful approach in understanding the value of changing the mind. Back to my **lesson 132.** I read from paragraph 7. **But healing is the gift of those who are prepared to learn there is no world, and can accept that lesson now.** [WB, pg 243] It makes sense that until I believe there is no world out there, I will maintain judgment and condemnation on those I feel victimized by. I sometimes think what I need to do is release the fear, and release wrong thoughts. But it is more than that. It is understanding that nothing really happened. It is having *zero judgment* on the wrong-minded thoughts. It is difficult though. I mean, how can you get your head around the idea that nothing just happened? That it was some kind of stage act. That no-one is really out there doing anything to me? This is going to take some convincing to shift my current awareness. My awareness tells me that this is very real. Somebody is out there. I can see them. I can hear them. I can even touch them! It sure seems convincing enough to me that there are people everywhere and they all appear very real. Wow. How long is this going to take? This unlearning of who I thought I was? And this unlearning of who I thought others were?

All fear occurs in the wrong mind, and all sickness is of the wrong mind. So…removing the fear that occupies the wrong mind removes the framework for sickness. I guess I know what I have to do; I just have to keep moving along here. The big message here is: Am I prepared to learn there is no world? In this lesson today Jesus is telling me that healing can occur for those who can accept that lesson now. I suppose I have to know that while I see the world as very real, and while I make every comment and every action very real then I will remain stuck.

There is no question. I must be brave enough to succumb to the idea that nobody is doing anything to me and accept that I am doing absolutely *everything* to myself. I feel myself getting tense at the largeness of this task. Just then, I feel this gentle urge rise from within, that says, "Relax and don't push yourself Robyn. We'll get there." I feel a comfort within now. The Voice is telling me to be patient and that all will unfold in its right time.

Moving on to paragraph 10.2 in today's lesson. **To free the world from every kind of pain is but to change your mind about yourself. There is no world apart from your ideas because ideas leave not their Source, and you maintain the world within your mind in thought.** [WB, pg 243] When I can understand that we are all in this together, I can then look to my brothers and cease complaints and judgments. For what I am giving to my brother I am giving to myself. Therefore, I am doing everything to myself. I recall Jesus' message in the Bible, "Forgive them father, for they know not what they do." It is simple: if I can't forgive myself I can't forgive my brother, then I stay in the wrong mind and the illusion lives on, sickness is a given, and waking up is but a distant memory.

I repeat my lesson. **I loose the world from all I thought it was.** I pause to consider... my brother doesn't want the pain anymore than I do. And someone has to make the first move here. Just as the tiki torch lights the path here in Maui, we must stand strong and light the path for our brother. I know it's not easy as we stretch up high, out of our comfort zone, to light it. But as we light the first torch the second torch gets easier and then the third. And soon the path is well lit, and the way home for me and my brother is clear.

As I head to Lahaina for lunch, I look at the world around me and **I loose the world from all I thought it was.** It feels good. As I step out into the small town of Lahaina, I realize how much I love this little town, but I also know in the back of my mind I can release this little town. A greater gift awaits me. I spend the rest of the day walking around, shopping, and just enjoying the feel of Lahaina. I found a place to eat right by the water and watched the sun as it slowly made its descent over the deep blue sea. And as I steadied my camera for an extraordinary sunset shot, I stopped for a second to remind myself that a greater gift awaits me. I then repeated my lesson. **I loose the world from all I thought it was.**

I WILL NOT VALUE WHAT IS VALUELESS

The early sky is a pretty pink on this new December morning. The sea is calm in that deep Hawaii blue. From my balcony I clearly see the island of Lanai in the distance revealing mountainous creases in its unpopulated land. I think I will visit there today. That sounds like a fun plan.

I finish my breakfast, gather a few things for my day trip, and head to Lahaina Harbor. As I approach the harbor the energy is cheery and uplifting while many scurry to chosen boats to embark on their adventures. The boat to Lanai is full of smiling people. I sit and chat to a lady who works at the Four Seasons on Lanai, who advises me that a mere 3,000 people reside on this island of 140.5 square miles. Wow, that's fewer than populate most towns back in LA! For example, Hermosa Beach is only 1.3 square miles and has a population of 20,000!

As we are about midway between Maui and Lanai screams are heard from the back of the boat. One girl points out to sea. I look to catch the tail end of a whale. Within minutes another one jumps clean out of the ocean. We counted five jumps in total. It is the beginning of whale season here in Hawaii. Yesterday I went on a whale watching tour and saw a mother and her calf frolicking in the warm Hawaiian waters just off Maui.

As I sit and look out to sea I realize that detachment has a lot of meaning for me right now. I find it hard to believe that this is an illusion when I see an animal such as a whale jumping clean out of the ocean, as though it is putting on a show just for us. It does make it feel very real. Or, could it be a message from Holy Spirit who is enjoying this journey and telling us it is okay to enjoy it too?

As we enter the harbor of Lanai the few boats reflect the sparse population which inhabits this island. And as I look out over the first hill that enters my vision there is not a building in sight.

The shuttle took us directly to the Four Seasons Hotel which sits high on a cliff-face overlooking the beautiful beach called Hulopoe'e. This beach is gorgeous. If I was ever truly tested on attaching myself to this illusion a beautiful beach could do the trick! However, glimpses of the light are slowly but surely opening my eyes to where I am heading. As I lay on a sun lounge on the cliff-top overlooking the beach below, I enjoy the beauty and then gently detach myself from it. I smile in the back of my mind, remembering the truth. Just months ago I felt sad when I had to remind myself that something beautiful wasn't real, but an illusion instead. Today I feel okay with enjoying the beauty and just seeing it for what it is—an illusion—which seems to naturally remove my attachment to it. I know this lovely island of Lanai is a beautiful picture, but I know in my heart that it isn't even close to the beautiful picture that resides blocked from my full awareness. Is this beauty before me then enough to stop me from moving forward to my Truth? I don't think so.

I take a moment to repeat my lesson for the day. **Lesson 133. I will not value what is valueless.** [WB, pg 245] I pause to consider the picturesque beach before me as I determine it as valueless. I relax as a couple of butterflies dance around the flowers in front of me. It is as though they have a message and are dancing for my benefit. They seem so happy and free, and detached from any concerns. It is a strong word— "detachment." If only we could detach ourselves from all our worries and all of our concerns. Hmm, that causes me to question, "Isn't every 'need' that we have an attachment to something or to an outcome?"

A friend asked me the other day, "What are your goals for the new year?" For the first time in a very long time I realized I have no goals. This friend that knew me quite well was surprised and said, "What do you mean you have no goals for 2008?" I thought about it and said, "I really don't have any. I feel inspired to take each day as it comes right now. Tomorrow, I may feel different. Tomorrow I may have a goal, I don't know...but I think I'll wait until one is offered to me. I don't feel the need to go looking for one today." I surprised myself in realizing this new outlook. I always had some goals lined up in my life. So this was so not like me but it felt good and it felt right. I knew that the Course had something to do with the way I was feeling. To have no attachment to the future felt good. I also felt very safe. This Inner Knowing tells me, "All will be fine. You have nothing to be concerned about. Just stay with me, I'll show you the way." I love the connection

I feel with Holy Spirit today. I do feel I am in safe hands. Each time I connect to the Truth via my daily lessons I feel grateful that this knowledge is growing stronger within me.

I pause to repeat my lesson. **I will not value what is valueless.** I stop and look at the beach below. This view below me is beautiful. It is even spectacular. If you've ever been to Lanai, you will know what I mean. Peace, beauty, colorful waters, stillness, and butterflies. But even this won't hold me back now. Not now that I am beginning to understand the truth. This is but a dream. It's a *very* pretty piece of the dream. But the dream isn't always pretty. Next week, something may surface where I am tested to stay connected. And then for sure I will turn to reach for the truth once again. I can't go back and forward like a yo-yo any longer. I have to make a final decision to wake up from this dream. I have to know in my heart that this is truly what I am wanting. I look around me and proclaim that what I see is valueless! It is. What can it give me tomorrow? What can I take with me except a memory? Will it make me feel good next week when I begin to disconnect over something else? Does it truly have anything to offer me? I have to see it for what it is and that is a pretty part of this dream. This dream that has many layers—layers that include rough edges, and layers that include smooth edges. There is good and there is ugly here in this dream. There is drama and there is peace. There is laughter and there are tears. There is duality, and I no longer choose this duality. I choose Love. I choose freedom. I won't be tricked just because something in front of me is breathtaking. Hmmm, *breathtaking* could also mean "here is some beauty to entice you to take another breath of the dream." It seems that there is always something that attaches us to this dream, like the continual, picturesque landmarks of Hawaii. I am beginning to get it. I am beginning to understand why I must detach myself from all of this. I must continually remind myself now that everything I see is *not* real. I can enjoy it. Yes. I can enjoy it all. But I can't make it real.

REFLECTING ON MY NEW PATH

I thoroughly enjoyed visiting the island of Lanai yesterday. And I have thoroughly enjoyed my time on Maui. Yet, tomorrow, I must leave the aloha spirit and head back to the mainland for Xmas. I am not sure how I feel about going back to the mainland. I feel so free here. I am able to continue along my path with no interruptions. I also feel that things will be different back home now with this new attitude I am developing about my surroundings. I wonder how it will affect my everyday life. I don't want to appear any different to my friends. However, I do want to continue along this new path, and for that reason I know I must take this new attitude home with me. I just feel uneasy about it for some reason. I am beginning to feel like a different person. A part of me wants to stay here in Maui and hide out for a while but I know I must face the music of change, whatever that change may bring to me. As that thought stirs within, this other Voice echoes through the silence of the moment that says, "Robyn, it will unfold perfectly. Relax, and go with the flow." Yes, I must have faith that Holy Spirit has a plan and that my path will unfold perfectly. I feel I have come so far already. I could never turn back. I have taken the "bull by the horns" so to speak. I stop and smile to myself. Hmm, no…it is the ego I have taken by the horns!

Chapter 6

Letting Him Lead the Way

OPENING THE DOOR

Now that the excitement of a new year has subsided it's back to normal life here in Southern California. Today is January 15, 2008. Holy Spirit has been on my mind a lot these past weeks. The more I pay attention to His Voice, the more familiar I become with the variables that exist between His Voice and the voice of fear. It feels good to know that God has given me pure, loving guidance to assist in removing the obstacles in my wrong mind.

It doesn't surprise me that my lesson for the day is **lesson 155. I will step back and Let Him lead the way.** [WB, pg 291] It seems so appropriate right now. I have been focusing more and more on receiving pure guidance from Holy Spirit. I look forward to the day when I can feel the presence of Holy Spirit in every step I take.

I continue with my lesson and feel moved as I read the first paragraph. **There is a way of living in the world that is not here, although it seems to be. You do not change appearance, though you smile more frequently. Your forehead is serene; your eyes are quiet. And the ones who walk the world as you do recognize their own. Yet those who have not yet perceived the way will recognize you also, and believe that you are like them, as you were before.**

Sometimes I think that enlightenment (waking up) means becoming alienated from everything I knew and everyone I loved. It helps to read this in my lesson today and accept that I can move forward knowing that the world will basically remain as is and my existence to others will not alter. Only my existence within will feel different.

It's a crisp, clear, beautiful morning. I grab my sun lotion and hat then jump in the car and head to the beach. As I take my morning walk along the beach, I pause to repeat my lesson. **I will step back and let Him lead the way.** I envision holding out my hand and Holy Spirit gently taking it and guiding me forward. I look up ahead and sense God in the distance. I envision Holy Spirit guiding me towards God. It feels good. In the next moment I realize that if I'm to hand over the reins entirely to Holy Spirit then I must be mindful of actually letting them go. We both can't hold the reins. I remember in that moment that I must give up control of *everything* if I'm to continue on this path. I cringe a little. I like to have my say at times. But I know in my heart that the only way to continue moving forward is to release the reins. Just now as I type this, or I should say, as the computer types this (for I am speaking into a microphone) it actually typed by mistake "release the brains," instead of "release the reins." I smile to myself. This work is kind of like releasing the brain. *Thinking* is our way of creating outcomes of our desires as I learned in PF1. If I take the reins I am controlling my outcome. I'm *thinking* my outcome into existence. When I release the focus/desire to decide for myself, I give up control, relax, and let Holy Spirit decide for me.

As the thought of handing over the reins entirely becomes more of a probability on my part, I suddenly recognize the faith I must endure. Not only must I be attentive to the different voices, and ensure I am *only* listening to the Voice for God, but I must trust Holy Spirit completely with *every* decision made on my behalf. Giving up control completely in every aspect of my life, and then having the faith in something that's invisible seems kind of insane. However, in ACIM it is kindly pointed out to me that the ego part of me, believing that I am *actually* here, is the one who is insane. I have read enough and come far enough to know that this is true. However, thankfully, I am sane enough to know that it is time to hand over the reins.

OTHER ENLIGHTENING MATERIAL

My girlfriend, Sira, recently gave me a book to read called *Spiritual Enlightenment*, by Jed McKenna. I have only known Sira for a year or so, but the day we met we instantly connected. Today we journey down this spiritual path together. We started the 365 Workbook lessons around the same time. It is fun to meet with her and discuss our journey. To this day, I don't think I have joined with another Course student who is more eager than Sira to reach the Light. It is wonderful to walk this path with a student who believes there is no turning back.

Jed's book, *Spiritual Enlightenment*, is a wonderful book, and one which I have had trouble putting down. There are some interesting points Jed makes along the way about enlightenment. In one chapter, Jed is being interviewed. The interviewer asks, "You're enlightened but you obviously still have ego, so isn't that a contradiction? Doesn't the ego have to be annihilated to achieve nirvana?" The same question had crossed my mind. So when I heard the interviewer's question I was interested in hearing Jed's answer. Jed said, "Good question. Both are true. Yes, I have an ego and it looks similar to the one I dropped, as you say, to achieve nirvana. But then I came back all enlightened and everything, and I needed something to wear. I look around and there's my discarded ego lying in a pile on the floor, so I slip into it and here I am. You've probably heard the saying, 'Before enlightenment a mountain is a mountain, during enlightenment a mountain is not a mountain, and after enlightenment a mountain is a mountain again.' Well it's like that. Before enlightenment, I believed my ego was me. Then enlightenment comes along and no more ego, only the underlying reality. Now it's after enlightenment and this ego might be slightly uncomfortable or ill-fitting at times, but it's all I've got."

In Jed's book, he offers such a lighthearted approach that enlightenment all of a sudden seems not only achievable, but not as scary and alien as it once did. That is great news! I must say, I have enjoyed sharing in Jed's personal approach toward enlightenment and have received some insightful information. As far as the journey toward enlightenment goes, Jed's approach is quite different from the Course's approach. However, I feel we are each on our own personal journey and being guided to what works best for each of us, so I do believe there is no right or wrong approach. Recently, I have heard some Course teachers advise that students are best to stick to the Course if they have chosen the Course as their path. Apparently, choosing more than one method may become a hindrance toward gaining the required results of the Course. I can understand how that might be the case. With that in mind, since I have chosen to undertake the 365 lessons and feel in my heart the Course is the right path for me today, I will make it a point to adhere to the Course's teachings today in my own personal journey. However, I do understand the

Course may not be the right path for everyone, there are other alternatives, and Jed's approach is one such example.

WHAT IS A MIRACLE?

When I picked up the Course again, 6 months ago, I wanted a clear definition of what a *miracle* means as far as the Course goes. In chapter one of the Text there are 50 points listed under "The meaning of Miracles," which I found very helpful. However, I also found this excerpt in the Workbook, which, in a nutshell, told me exactly what I needed to hear: **A miracle is a correction. It does not create, nor really change at all. It merely looks on devastation, and reminds the mind that what it sees is false. It undoes error, but does not attempt to go beyond perception, nor exceed the function of forgiveness. Thus it stays within time's limits. Yet it paves the way for the return of timelessness and love's awakening, for fear must slip away under the gentle remedy it brings.** [WB, pg 473, 1.1] At the time, after reading this excerpt, I came to realize that when I do a forgiveness lesson I am releasing the wrong-minded thought by forgiving it, and then the *miracle* would appear in the way of a correction to that aspect of my wrong mind. I knew at that point if I was serious about removing all wrong-minded thinking then I must learn how to forgive in the way that the Course would have me forgive. However, back then I didn't have a full understanding of how to *forgive* via the means of the Course, nor do I today actually. I am still grasping the art of handing over the wheel completely. And on top of that I am grasping the art of joining with my brother. Both still seem like a distance away right now. It does feel like I am taking baby steps, but I have come to realize that I have no choice. Baby steps are what I must take. While I am in control—meaning judging and feeling like a victim at times—it seems almost impossible to even begin to forgive my brother. I guess that I have to be patient and allow this to unfold as it will. I will only hinder myself if I get upset that miracles are not occurring in my life at this time.

An interesting point is that in PF1 I would take responsibility for all that my brother appeared to do to me, because I understood from Law of Attraction that I had attracted (via complaining) what my brother had done. So I knew from releasing the complaint (victimized thought) that I would release the same event manifesting once again. It worked. I found much harmony in my life from doing this and from taking responsibility for my wrong-minded, complaining thoughts. However, after I started the Course, I felt a gentle nudge from Holy Spirit to cease doing that, and instead, allow the wrong-minded thoughts to surface—which would enable me to learn how to look at them differently today in PF2. I have come to understand that when I release the complaining thought about my brother (PF1), the thought will lie dormant and no longer attract, but it will not be healed. So, in other words, the thought is being swept under the mat so to speak and ignored instead. But it seems that when we move into PF2, and take it a step further and *forgive* our brother then the ill thought is now *seen* differently, not just disregarded. Our "understanding" about our brother's action has now changed. We no longer make that action real.

I think it is important that today I do choose miracles; however, it is not important at this point if miracles are occurring in my life or not. They will be mine as I learn to forgive in line with the Course, and also at the right time. Again, I must be patient. I am learning tenfold just how important *patience* really is on this journey.

QUESTIONING THE COURSE

One question that had passed through my mind not long after becoming a student of the Course was, "Once we wake up from this dream, how do we know that we will not fall asleep and dream another dream?" I understand this is coming from the ego, however, at the time, being a new Course student, a valid question considering there is much ego to undo. Upon reading the Text again and coming across this paragraph my heart felt lifted as this answer rang true for me. **The Voice of the Holy Spirit is the Call to Atonement, or the restoration of the integrity of the mind. When the Atonement is complete and the whole Sonship is healed there will be no Call to return. But what God creates is eternal. The Holy Spirit will remain with the Sons of God, to bless their creations and keep them in the light of joy.** [Text, pg 74, 5.4] Once the atonement is complete Holy Spirit will remain with us to bless our creations and *keep* us in the light of joy. Halleluiah! "Ask and you shall receive." I love that. Each time I have a question it is not long before the answer is revealed.

When I look back to the beginning of the Course lessons I recall questioning the thought of letting go of all that I had previously learned. However, today, the Course continues to reveal to me that I do not know all I thought I knew. So now I move forward learning to have faith in releasing a lifetime of knowledge and trusting that Holy Spirit has eternal knowledge ready for me—the knowledge I once knew before I fell asleep. Today, I came across this excerpt from the Course which I found interesting: **Yet the essential thing is learning that *you do not know.* Knowledge is power, and all power is of God. You who have tried to keep power for yourself have "lost" it. You still have the power, but you have interposed so much between it and your awareness of it that you cannot use it.** [Text, pg 296, 1.1] This confirms yet again that there is no use in me holding on to that steering wheel. I don't know the way. And I surely don't know the answers. Holy Spirit knows the way, and Holy Spirit has every answer ready for me to hear when I am ready to listen. If only I would let go of the steering wheel and trust Holy Spirit entirely...it is then that I will be reminded of my true power.

Chapter 7

The Light of the Holy Relationship

A LESSON IN FORGIVENESS

The new year is moving by fast. It is 25th February already. A couple of weeks ago I placed my home in Redondo Beach on the market. I am not sure where I am moving to yet; however, I am planning on traveling to Hawaii for 2 months to spend some time writing. I guess after that I will come back to the South Bay and rent for a while. My finances are not so abundant right now and the housing market isn't doing so well with the economic downturn, so it seems a good time to sell my home. And on top of that, a feeling I get tells me it is the right time to move on from this location.

This past weekend at an open home I was truly tested with forgiveness. Saturday afternoon I held my home open for buyers. Toward the end of the day a family walked through. They were a husband and wife in their mid 40's, and a boy who appeared to be about 18 years of age. While the woman continued chatting to me in the living room, the boy disappeared into my bedroom and the man disappeared into my spare room. After they left, something felt weird about the way they had viewed my home. When I checked the rooms, I found open boxes and items loosely lying around on the floor. Well, to make a long story short, they stole some jewelry, and the items they took were sentimental. I had actually removed some valuable jewelry one week prior, however, I had forgotten about these sentimental pieces in the lower drawers of a cabinet in my bedroom.

As soon as I realized what had happened, I knew that this was going to be another one of those forgiveness lessons. I was surprised at how quickly I recognized the lesson and opportunity for forgiveness. It showed me that my work was beginning to pay off. However, with that being said, I still felt a desire to see these people punished.

I began to consider my feelings about the stolen jewelry and asked myself why I felt so upset. I recalled the work I had done in Hawaii regarding attachment versus detachment. Who needs things and who attaches itself to things? The ego of course! I wondered why *things* become sentimental. Why do we feel this way? I realized it was a decision that I had made somewhere along the way that created an attachment to these pieces of jewelry. To acknowledge the attachment felt good. And to acknowledge that I could indeed detach myself felt even better.

I also realized in the moment that the only way to feel better about the situation was to become detached from the feelings I had about these people. I decided I could keep reminding myself to just "let it go." But the Voice within said no, that won't cut it. If you forget about it, or just let it go, as in PF1, it will silence the wrong-minded thought that attracted the situation; however, it will not *heal* that same wrong-minded thought that attracted the situation.

I asked Holy Spirit for assistance in understanding how I could heal and feel better. The feeling that came to me said, "You must be able to think about these people and join with them."

I realized this was my opportunity to "forgive." And if I didn't accept it and do the work, then I would only fall back toward the darkness instead of moving forward toward the Light. I held a visual of the people in my mind and tried to see through to their goodness—that of the Sonship. That's when it dawned on me. It wasn't the Sonship in them that robbed me, but instead it was their ego that had robbed me. And who was their ego robbing? Their ego was robbing my ego!

THE SON IS BORN IN SINLESSNESS

This morning, I sit down to complete my lesson for the day. I am up to **lesson 181**. And as soon as I begin reading I smile to myself. **I trust my brothers, who are one with me.** [WB, pg 337] I read on to paragraph 1.2. **When you attack a brother, you proclaim that he is limited by what you have perceived in him. You do not look beyond his errors. Rather, they are magnified, becoming blocks to your awareness of the Self that lies beyond your own mistakes, and past his seeming sins as well as yours.**

I read on to paragraph 2. **Perception has a focus. It is this that gives consistency to what you see. Change but this focus, and what you behold will change accordingly. Your vision now will shift, to give support to the intent which has replaced the one you held before. Remove your focus on your brother's sins, and you experience the peace that comes from faith in sinlessness.**

Throughout the day, when I am unable to trust my brother, I am then to repeat: *It is not this that I would look upon. I trust my brothers who are one with me.* [WB, pg 338, 6.4]

65

As I begin my lesson the first thought that comes to my mind is of course the people who stole at the open home. Throughout the day they enter my mind again and again. When the mistrust and pain surfaces within I repeat... ***It is not this that I would look upon. I trust my brothers who are one with me.***

I was working at seeing through to the Sonship in them and bypassing the ego. Though for some reason it wasn't always working. Sometimes I would find it quite difficult to do. Then I remembered something that came to me in meditation a few days ago. I was asking Holy Spirit to reveal my Identity as the Son of God. Let me see if I can explain what I felt. It was as though my Spirit all of a sudden extended far out to the horizon but a weird thing happened—it didn't stop. I could feel an unending feeling that somehow continued on forever. I felt no containment. I felt the freedom of a continual loving energy. It felt amazing. It then began to feel very normal, and no longer weird. It felt natural to have no ending. I know this may sound quite bizarre. But that is truly how it felt. Then it dawned on me that this feeling I was being shown was in fact a feeling that presents itself when we become *One* as the Sonship. If the bodies were gone, then all that would be left is an extension of Love. One Being. One Mind. The ego would no longer be present. That was my first experience in realizing that my brother could actually be "me." That was an amazing moment.

So, today, I decided to revisit this feeling as I did in meditation. I began to feel my Spirit extend from my body. I felt the truth and the love of my Existence. Then I felt myself extend onward forever. That is when it became easier to release my anger toward these people and feel myself extend through them and beyond them. In the next moment I felt that I was *one* with them. It felt really good. On Saturday I didn't know if I would ever be able to see them in a good healthy light, nor if I really wanted to for that matter. However, this new feeling I have found today is quite incredible.

Each time, during the day, I would repeat my lesson and then think of these people. I initially found it difficult. I still felt remorse and anger toward them. However, after quickly reminding myself to join with them as the Sonship and following the steps I had learned in meditation, I soon found the bad feelings dissipating.

The forgiven are the means of the Atonement. Being filled with spirit, they forgive in return. Those who are released must join in releasing their brothers, for this is the plan of the Atonement. [Text, pg 9, 3.1]

I pause to repeat my lesson one more time before I go to bed. **I trust my brothers, who are one with me.** I can almost feel that I am moving forward and progressing with some level of forgiveness. Am I all the way? Most definitely not. Though, I have a feeling that this is the beginning of a forgiveness that will increase with time.

I don't want to blame and judge my brothers, no matter who they are or what they are doing to me. I want to heal the wrong-minded thoughts of the ego. And I am learning more as each day passes the only way to do that is to continue practicing "forgiveness." So that is what I am going to do.

JOINING IN THE HOLY LIGHT

Understanding "oneness" at the level of the Course is a task in itself. I pray to have the strength and courage to work at joining with my brother in every step that offers me the lesson. I feel that this is the depth of the Course. For it enables me to forgive my brother each time I join with him. Joining is a vital step, for it is "joining" that promotes the will to forgive.

When I can join in a relationship and practice forgiveness for the purpose of waking up, then that relationship will become a holy relationship. These past few days I have spent some time considering the idea of holy relationships. I found this following excerpt in the Text:

Think what a holy relationship can teach! Here is belief in differences undone. Here is the faith in differences shifted to sameness. And here is sight of differences transformed to vision. Reason now can lead you and your brother to the logical conclusion of your union. It must extend, as you extended when you and he joined. It must reach out beyond itself, as you reached out beyond the body, to let you and your brother be joined. And now the sameness that you saw extends and finally removes all sense of differences, so that the sameness that lies beneath them all becomes apparent. Here is the golden circle where you recognize the Son of God. For what is born into a holy relationship can never end. [Text, pg 467, 4.1]

As I see the Sonship in my brother, I see the Sonship in myself. This is where we unite, thus creating a golden circle where the Truth is recognized. I have decided that for me to move toward the Light then I must work at seeing my brother as myself. If I don't work at seeing my brother as myself then I will stay stuck and remain oblivious to the Truth. When I can see my brother as me, then my relationship with my brother will change from what I always knew, and become a holy relationship. That is what I want. I want union. I want peace and happiness. And I can only receive that when I join with my brother. So this means no more judgment. Hmm, appears easy to do. However, I know that judgment is a huge part of the wrong mind. We only know to judge. We only know how to make things right or wrong—good or bad. But while I judge I separate, and while I separate I stay stuck. Wow, this is some journey. The understanding required to even begin to walk the path toward waking up goes so much against what I ever could have imagined!

I can tell that awareness is a key factor here. If I am *aware* then I can begin to catch myself judging. But then I have to "learn how to forgive what I am judging." And only then will the relationship begin to become a holy one. Wow, this sounds like quite the task.

In the past few days, I have been thinking of Mother Teresa and considering her responses and ways with people. I guess the thought of holy relationships has brought her to my mind. I never really knew much about her, however, I have seen some television coverage, and when I think of unconditional love I have found myself thinking of Mother Teresa. A holy relationship is an unconditional relationship. We learned of Jesus as an unconditional being, and we learned of Mother Teresa as an unconditional being—or in other words enlightened beings. In understanding that we must walk in their shoes hits home in why this appears to be such a task that lies ahead!

As I consider the largeness of this task, I stop to ponder my ability to walk this path. Can I do this? I really don't know. But I do know that I will have to be patient with myself, and be okay when I judge and screw up. I do want the freedom and happiness that I know is my gift. I do wish to see others with loving eyes as Mother Teresa did. And I do wish to encounter holy relationships.

CHANGES ON THE HORIZON

Lessons 201-220 are review lessons. I am at **lesson 214** today [WB, pg 394]. At each review lesson, I am to start and end the lesson by repeating, **I am not a body. I am free. For I am still as God created me.** My review lesson today is: **I place the**

future in the Hands of God. Today's lesson reaffirms my feelings about handing the wheel over to Holy Spirit, therefore placing my future in the hands of God. Since handing over the steering wheel a number of months ago, Holy Spirit has proven to me again and again that He surely does know how to steer this ship better than me. For example, remember how I told you I "felt guidance" to rip up that list of what I desired in a soul-mate? Well, going back to this past New Year's Eve. I had been to a party with a girlfriend. When we left the party, we got separated and I ended up missing my ride home. It was cold, late, and cabs were extremely scarce being New Years Eve. So I wandered up the street for a bit, and after a while I saw a cab waiting at the curbside. As I approached the cab it was empty. I was about to jump in when a man walked into view and said, "Hey, this is my cab! He then smiled and said, "We can share it though if you like," and then jumped in alongside me. Along the way we chatted and exchanged contact information. In the weeks that followed we emailed each other, however, we didn't make a plan to get together as each of us thought the other really wasn't all that interested. We found out later that both of us were in fact interested, but neither of us were the pushy kind and so just let things be. Then...on February 14th, Valentine's Day, it happened again. Another chance meeting was aligned in the Universe. Sparks were flying and we spent the evening shooting some pool and getting to know each other. It all felt right. So that was the beginning of our relationship. His name is Ian, and we have now been dating about 2 months.

Holy Spirit did a great job with that steering wheel! For the most part, what Ian has to offer wasn't even on that list I had prepared. He is a great guy, with great qualities; however, *his* qualities were not the ones I had in mind. In fact, if I were to continue to visualize *my* "perfect mate," instead of ripping up that list, I don't think Ian and I would have the chance of meeting today. So, I am very happy I ripped up that list and let Holy Spirit decide for me!

Today, things are going well with Ian and me. We enjoy each other a lot. However...I sold my house the other day, and after escrow closes, I am off to Hawaii for that 2 month trip I was telling you about. This is going to be interesting. Holy Spirit has done a nice job so far with the steering wheel, so I am not going to interfere. I am just going to do what "feels" right. And it feels right to keep my plans for Hawaii. So I guess we'll see how this unfolds. I must say, I haven't connected with a guy like this in ages. However, a feeling tells me to trust Holy Spirit and continue with my current plans. So trust Holy Spirit I will!

Chapter 8

Return to Paradise

IS IT TIME TO GO HOME?

Today is the 11th June. I pause from my writing and pull an icy bottle of water from the cooler beside me. I am laying on one of the most picturesque beaches in the world—Lanikai Beach, Oahu.

It seems that Holy Spirit is saying, "Ok, let's take Robyn back to Hawaii again and again until she learns to detach herself from this dream!" After my last trip to Maui, I found myself getting caught up in the hustle and bustle of life again within the dream, back home in California. The thought of everything being just a dream quickly dissipated as if I had been told some farfetched fairy-tale.

It appears that over and over again a wake-up call is required to actually wake-up! And Hawaii is the place to offer me that I suppose—a place where I can relax and allow Holy Spirit to actually get through to me. Hawaii offers some of the most picturesque scenery in the world. It is a place where I can be delighted and then reminded yet again that this is one big fat dream.

My lesson today is **lesson 254. Let every voice but God's be still in me.** [WB, pg 421] It is amazing when I realize just how much the ego really does speak to me. After all, is it not my ego that indulges in the beauty of Lanikai...and in the beauty of this dream? Jed McKenna says in his book that people don't realize they are actually on a stage playing out their part in this dream. Hmm, it seems that people are like puppets and someone is pulling their strings. So, my question is, "How much of a say do we really have then?" Sometimes, I do wonder whether it would be better to just go back to PF1 and dream up this dream as good as I can. But the thought to return to PF1 doesn't last long. In the next instant this Voice usually follows that gently says, "You can do this Robyn. Relax for now and then move forward when you are ready."

I consider my boyfriend, Ian, who I have been missing a lot. We have such great times together. We even discuss the idea that this is all a dream together. He tells me how he wants to stay in this dream forever. And in that moment when I am laying in his arms I feel the same way. Then I begin to wonder what might happen when our lives end this lifetime? If we decide to stay in this dream, then I suppose we come back and do it all over again? And if we do, then what? I ponder the thought. Do I want to come back and start a new life? It was difficult at times going through school, dealing with exams, teachers, and each other's ego's. When I was a child I felt trapped. My soul wanted to be free. My soul wanted to fly. Then I recall times in my early adult years when I didn't understand life, and I didn't understand the laws of attraction." When I didn't know how to create well, and I didn't have a clue why life got difficult at times.

But, then, there were some great times too. I was blessed as a child to have the freedom of climbing trees, running through paddocks, collecting tadpoles, and anything that crawled or flew that I could fit inside my "bug catcher." And then there are those romantic times when it seems as though life couldn't get any better. But even when times are really good it seems that somewhere, not too far away, something is going to happen to make me go, "Oh shit."

When I consider Ian and the love we share together, I then ask myself, "What do I possibly know about the future?" We really only have this moment in time to enjoy. We don't know what is in store for us. But on the upside, we can make the most of this lifetime and continue to enjoy each other while we undo the ego right? Well, I can only speak for myself. Ian will make that decision when he is ready...or not. That is okay. A feeling tells me that it doesn't matter what he decides, all that matters is what I decide for me.

Ian and I discuss the Course together. When we have difficulty and the ego comes out we talk about it. We recognize that it is a false experience that we are having. It is not real. To discuss the Course with him is a lot of fun. Ian likes to test me on it. He offers reasons to stay in the dream. I love that. I love being with someone who gets it, and who understands the Course, yet tests the truth in it. It makes me look at this closely and know in my heart what it is that I truly want. We have some great conversations.

I pause to repeat my lesson, **Let every voice but God's be still in me.** I ponder this lesson for a few minutes and then ask, "Why would I come home to you God? Tell me, why is it better there than here?

I do want to remember my Truth. My heart tells me I am on track, and that it is time to go home. But even though I feel in my heart that this is true, I still don't know what I am going home to. I want a glimpse, a taste, a memory. As I write, something says to me, "Just keep going Robyn, and keep doing what you are doing. As darkness is removed, Light will enter, and you will begin to remember. For now, keep seeking to release the ego."

I still find it difficult to believe one hundred percent that this is a dream. Sometimes I think I'm sold on the fact that it is one, and then other times I stop and go, "Nah, it can't be!" When I practiced PF1, I recall thinking this is ALL real. I remember learning that there is love and there is fear. And just get rid of the fear and all will be perfect on this earth. But then how much of "what we perceive to be love" on this earth is actually true love? We often think that making another happy all the time is being giving, and is being loving to them, but isn't it really just pleasing the ego? Isn't it really just keeping the ego alive? As I ponder this thought, I realize that that is what this dream is all about. It's all about keeping the ego alive. Isn't everything in the dream to feed the ego? All material possessions really do feed the ego. Even some of the kind things we do for people, like listening to someone complain and moan, and we say, "There, there." It's just another form of feeding the ego. So, now I get it. What we're really doing is keeping the dream...therefore the ego, alive!

LESSONS ARE EVERYWHERE

Today's lesson is **lesson 255. This day I choose to spend in perfect peace.** [WB, pg 422] To do today's lesson and spend the day in perfect peace, I have to *continually* be aware of releasing the ego. Earlier today, I was parking in Waikiki, and a lady got upset at me when I stopped alongside her driveway. I was waiting for someone to move out of their parking spot in front of me, and I didn't realize I was blocking this lady from exiting her driveway. When she got upset at me (by tooting on her horn and giving me a disapproving look) I became frustrated and returned the annoyed glance. Then I remembered my lesson and instantly knew my peace was just taken away as I let this moment ruffle my egoic feathers. She doesn't realize that this is a dream. She thinks this is all very real. I sank in my seat. I had let the ego get the better of me. I wanted to offer a different message. So in the next moment, as she pulled out of the driveway, I turned to offer her an approving look and smile. I could tell this utterly confused her. I felt warm inside, and was glad that I realized in enough time to change my mind and offer a different message...one of peace.

Right now I am relaxing in my friend's backyard (where I am currently staying) in Hawaii-Kai, looking out over a canal with its backdrop being a small hill of lava rock. My mind travels to a question I was thinking about earlier today. Who am I really? Yes, I know, the Sonship. But for now, until my memory returns, I don't feel like I'm the Sonship. As I sit here, I don't remember my Truth. Sure, I have had slight glimpses of something more. However, I have to accept that today, until I wake up, the mind I am operating from is ego. I suppose Jesus does mention in the Course that Holy Spirit is using "the wrong mind" to get me out of this dream.

I feel an inner, gentle knowing that Holy Spirit is smiling on me right now. A feeling surfaces that tells me, "As you come to realize how you are caught in this ego experience, and when you cease making it so real, is when you will begin to feel your Truth shine through. When the dream is over, Love is what is left. In the meantime, Love just sits back and waits. It is gentle. It doesn't have to push. And all you need to do today is be peaceful, calm, and just listen for the answers."

Ian and I had a conversation yesterday about the fear we have of each other's ego. We talked about how we are going to handle that in our relationship. We are both strong and independent people, and when one of our egos comes out, it tests the other one. We discussed how we are going to work at knowing when the other person (in their egoic stride) is not acting from their truth. So, we are going to work at staying connected. And when one of us can do that, then that person can assist the other person out of their egoic mood.

Just then a gentle Voice surfaces that says, "Well, Robyn, that is useful for staying in the dream and making it nice and cozy. You see how easy it is to get caught up in pleasing or softening each other's ego?"

Hmm, I didn't see it that way. So where am I going wrong here? I don't understand. I begin to feel flustered in trying to understand where I am going wrong and can no longer connect to hear the gentle Voice speaking to me. A long day it has been, so I think I will call it a day.

THE WAY TO GOD IS THROUGH FORGIVENESS

I find that I have to keep reminding myself daily that forgiveness is the way out. However, it is not always easy to know what requires forgiveness and what doesn't. Toward the end of last year, I fell and hurt my back. I was left with some lower disc protrusion and was given treatment for a few months. On occasion it still hurts and this morning it has been sore. Earlier, I stood up to soothe it while reading my lesson. Today I am at **lesson 256. God is the only goal I have today.** [WB, pg 422] And the first line is: **The way to God is through forgiveness here.** As I stood to stretch my back and complete my lesson I realized that forgiveness relates to everything here. Absolutely everything! So, I stopped and said to myself, "I am not going to make this pain in my back real. This is a dream. My back does not hurt." I then released the thought, sat down, and returned to my writing. It is now about three hours later, and I just realized something. I have not had any back pain at all since saying that forgiveness lesson! I forgave the pain, saw it as nothing but a crazy part of this dream, and then it went away! Now I know what to do. The next time I think my back has pain I won't join in the complaint because it simply isn't true! Complaining is of the ego. And I have to remember that every time I have a complaint, then I must do a forgiveness lesson on whatever it is that I am complaining about.

I really like today's lesson. It is so important for me to be reminded about forgiveness. It seems that forgiveness really is the way home. If I could define the meaning of forgiveness as I now know it, I would say it is taking an illusionary thought that I previously made real, and then telling my mind that it is no longer real—which then provides the space for Truth to enter. I smile and turn to my lesson. I read from the first paragraph. **God is our goal; forgiveness is the means by which our minds return to Him at last.** [WB, pg 422, 1.9] I always thought of forgiveness as letting something go that bothers me, and now I see it in a whole new light. It isn't only letting something go; forgiveness is *changing* my mind from wrong mind to Right Mind. Forgiveness is the answer to waking up.

FORGIVING MY SENSES

It is a pretty morning here in Hawaii-Kai. As I go about my day today I find it is difficult to remember forgiveness. It seems so easy to get caught up in normal day to day events and continue to make the dream real. I ponder my lesson today, **Lesson 257. Let me remember what my purpose is.** [WB, pg 423] I realize that throughout the day I am used to looking at my surroundings and making them very real. How can I forgive everything that I thought was real if I am still making it very real? I am finding that it is not so easy to look around me at everything I have made real for an entire lifetime and say "Oh, it's just a dream, so let me see this differently."

In part II of my Workbook lessons, there are 14 "Themes of Special Relevance" that I must review, one at a time, as specified, prior to completing my daily lesson. Today's "Theme of Special Relevance" is number **4. What is sin?** I read from the first paragraph. **Sin gave the body eyes, for what is there the sinless would behold? What need have they of sights or sounds or touch? What would they hear or reach to grasp? What would they sense at all? To sense is not to know. And truth can be but filled with knowledge, and with nothing else.** [WB, pg 419, 1.4]

Wow, so even my senses I must forgive! I always thought that my senses held many answers. Now I must tell myself that I don't know what I thought I knew in almost every area of my life! All of a sudden I feel as though I have been living in a tiny dark room. And the Truth lived outside of this room. I guess the only answer now is that I must listen to the Voice as often as I can. The Voice has the answers. Not my senses. Wow, we have trusted in our senses for so long. But I suppose that senses are really a part of the body, and the body is really just a puppet in this dream.

As I get used to the idea that this is just a dream—a bunch of baloney—I suppose I must wander around in the dark and keep trying to find that light switch. I don't recall anyone mentioning where the light switch was? Wouldn't that be cool if someone came along and said, "Oh, here's the light switch over here!" Then they turned it on, and we wake up all of a sudden and see the Light! But I suppose that we have to "decide that we no longer choose fear." This feeling inside tells me that we have to choose Love over fear again and again and again, before the Light is able to reveal itself. We have ignored the Light for so many different reasons. Because of that fear stands in our way for all those reasons. Those reasons need to be forgiven now. And they can only be forgiven when we turn to choose Love instead.

Removing this knowledge that I have known for a whole lifetime is not easy, but I realize that this is what I must do if I want to begin to see the Light. And I must *continually* remind myself that this is a dream. Every day, and in every moment, I must remind myself that this is just one big fat dream!

Chapter 9

Recognizing my Goal

TAKING A CLOSER LOOK AT JUDGMENT

Ian and I are basically continuing our relationship via Skype while I am here in Hawaii. We make a date each evening to see each other. It is a fun way to continue the relationship. He is actually visiting here in two weeks time. I can't wait. Today, however, I have been dwelling on a few things. When I am not in a romantic relationship I find that everything seems to go a lot smoother. Not so much seems to surface to cause pain or discomfort. Ian and I are both strong people, which I love. However, we both put our points across and don't hold anything back, and I know that we can both be as butt-headed and egoic as each other at times.

This feeling begins to emerge that tells me, "When you are focused on going home, Robyn, relationships will come to you that assist you in going home. These relationships do this by the forgiveness opportunities they present. When you understand this then you will appreciate your relationships all the more."

Okay, but I don't see how I can continually see Ian in a good light and stop a judgment from surfacing? It is difficult when I make an uncomfortable event real.

Straight away a feeling surfaces again that tells me, "Work at seeing Ian as the holy Son of God. He is really *you*, Robyn. See the Sonship in Ian and join with that part of him. You give the ego too much credit each time it surfaces in your conversations. Just keep reminding yourself how false the ego is. Keep working at seeing the Sonship in Ian and join with that."

Okay, I will work at seeing Ian as the holy Son of God and work on my forgiveness. I understand that I must do this if I want to remember the Truth and witness peace and love every day. And I believe we can have that in our relationship. As I sit here pondering this thought, I am reminded of a sentence I read a few weeks ago in the Workbook, under the first Theme of Special Relevance, **1. What is Forgiveness?** The sentence is: **Forgiveness recognizes what you thought your brother did to you has not occurred.** [WB, pg 401, 1.1]

As I take a closer look at our relationship and the pain that sometimes surfaces, I come to the realization that there is one true and very solid answer as to why we feel hurt at times. And that answer can be summed up in one word..."judgment." Every time something hurts, I have a choice. I can choose Love or I can choose pain. If I unconsciously make the choice to feel pain, I then instantly begin to make a clear judgment on why this thing hurts, thus the pain continues. It is becoming very clear to me why *A Course in Miracles* is a book about forgiveness. Because that is truly the *only* other choice I have when I wish to completely heal/remove pain. I can either judge the situation or the person, or I can sit back and realize that this is only a dream, that this person is me, and then release the thought as being false and unreal. When I can see it as a dream it is easy to just let the pain go. What I am really doing is forgiving the pain because now I see it differently. I am no longer making it real.

It is making more sense to me now. When we take away meaning, we take away judgment. To have no judgment means to have no attachment. So, true forgiveness is the removal of all judgment while *accepting* something exactly as it is and having zero judgment now or ever!

I take a look at life and realize in every moment I have choice, and this can relate to absolutely *everything* in my surroundings, and that choice is, "Am I going to choose ego, or am I going to choose God? Or, am I going to choose fear, or am I going to choose Love? In other words, am I going to judge and make real, or am I going to forgive?"

THE VOID OF LOVE

Relationships won't fulfill what we are *all* searching for—the freedom, pure happiness, and ongoing peace. For a while they may appear to offer us these things, but they can't fill the void we have within—the void of Love. We are all searching for *something* to fill that void. Be it a relationship, material possessions, or consumption. It doesn't matter what it is. Many of us unconsciously hope that each new thing that enters our existence will help to fill that ongoing void that we feel within.

I realize today that my relationship is not going to provide the *true* happiness that I am searching for. My relationship with Ian is very important to me. He is a blessing. However, there is something I have to realize. I have to realize that this relationship is assisting me to wake up. If Ian is me, then I must realize that we are One, and that we are here together, to assist each other to wake up and see the Truth.

It is almost sad. However, I know that I can't make this relationship of the ego world more important than going home. Otherwise, I will stay stuck in this ongoing battle with ego. And I must make the Sonship in Ian more important than anything. It seems like such a mountain to climb if I am to see Ian as someone other than the person that I have come to know and adore within this dream, and to overlook certain aspects of him that seem to make up who he is. It feels almost demeaning to his character to no longer see him as the person that he appears to be! But as I take a breath here, I realize that this is the ego talking. The ego part of me wants me to see it this way, so then maybe, just maybe, I will change my mind and decide to stay in this dream!

THE SONSHIP ONLY SMILES

It is the ego that points the finger, and says, "You have done wrong." Who has done wrong? Isn't it the ego that tells the ego he has done wrong? Can we point the finger at the Sonship? Not really, because the Sonship would only smile and realize the ego isn't real. The Sonship would say, "This is not true, the one who is pointing the finger is not real." So, I have to remember that each time I am feeling hurt it is my ego that is hurt, and whatever has hurt my ego can't be real. Only the ego attacks. The Sonship doesn't attack. So rather than getting upset and pointing the finger, I can choose to say, "That wasn't real. If it were real, it could only be a loving comment or action."

In a majority of relationships we are dealing with the ego most of the time. We might think otherwise but the ego plays most of the roles in relationships. In a romantic relationship, who is falling in love, really? It can't be the Sonship, the Sonship already loves everyone. It doesn't need to fall in love. The ego needs "special love" and "special relationships." The Sonship needs nothing at all. The Sonship is pure Love to begin with. Everything that the ego "takes" is to fill a void. It fills the void where Love is missing. The ego *needs* things. It needs possessions, relationships, houses, cars etc. The ego "needs" to survive.

When we can understand this, then we can turn around and say "I choose Love." I am seeing more clearly now that we have to understand how the ego operates in our lives before we can ask for the opposite. We have to know fear before we can ask for Love. And when we ask for Love we're really asking to remember who we are. But how can we remember who we are when the ego has done a nice cover-up job? It is beginning to make sense that the fast track to removing the ego has to be forgiveness.

It is obvious to me now that while we continue to idolize relationships, houses and cars, etc., we will keep ourselves from waking up. It takes a removal of the importance of all these things for us to be able to rise above the *neediness* of the ego. Sure, we can enjoy these things, but there is a fine line between enjoying...and attaching.

I think many of us understand that all material possessions can do for us is in fact fill a void, but what about a romantic relationship? It seems the ego has done a great cover-up on that one. I see Ian, and know that there is a greater part to him. I see the ego, acknowledge his ego, even love his ego, but I can also see aspects of the Sonship within him—the purity, the godliness, the bliss, the truth. However, as soon as I fall back into any kind of pain, I am quick to point the finger, and then I am looking at his false identity again—which is my false identity. When I can just see the ego for what it is and also see it in myself (for there is one wrong mind) then I can release it and go back deeper to that purer part of him and discover *more* of the Sonship, and more of my loving self, in him.

DIFFICULTY IN COMPLETING THE LESSONS

I now just finished a long walk along the white, sandy, 5 mile shoreline of Waimanalo Beach. The water is turquoise and inviting here, like many other gorgeous spots along the East Coast of Oahu. I look out over these pretty colored waters, while picking up my lesson, and wonder why I find it difficult at times to remember my lesson. I relax a minute and allow my lesson to soak in. **Lesson 258. Let me remember that my goal is God.** [WB, pg 423] The day has passed by. It is 5:40 p.m., and I have remembered my lesson only a few times today. Besides that I question myself as to how much I am implementing it. As I look back on the day I know I have judged certain things, made them real and important, and forgotten what my goal was. Why is it difficult at times to remember this simple goal? It's not as though I don't wish to witness the Truth and head home. I just seem to get lost in the humdrum of everyday life.

This feeling surfaces from within, "Robyn, you expect so much of yourself. You will get good at remembering, but for now this dream still seems very real to you. You have to keep telling yourself that it's a dream. It is the only way out. When you start to really believe (because right now, you don't) that this is a dream, that it's false, that it isn't real, then you will be able to dismiss things and make them meaningless. But right now, you still believe everything you see, everything you hear, and everything you touch. It is all very real to you. Look at your lesson, on page 419, **'What is sin?'** Your senses are telling you that the illusion is real right now. Your senses haven't changed 'course' yet. But they will. And when they do, then you can begin to catch yourself 'making the dream real.' Then you will remember your goal. Be easy on yourself, Robyn. The ego has many operating guises within the dream. You just have to realize which ones are ego. Each time you actually catch yourself and then refrain from seeing something as you once thought it was, you are taking yourself one step closer to home."

I break from my writing to repeat my lesson. **Let me remember that my goal is God.** I consider how often I have felt God's presence today. Maybe half a dozen times, at most. How many times would I consider God, if I did it on the hour, every hour? Let's say, 8 a.m. until 7 p.m., that makes it a dozen times. See, I am still judging myself where the lessons are concerned. Holy Spirit could talk to me a dozen times Himself, and I would still be judging myself! If I am not judging myself for the amount of times I have repeated the lesson, then I will judge myself on whether I did the lesson well or not! It is interesting how the ego sneaks in a guilty feeling wherever it possibly can. Well, I guess at least I am beginning to catch myself judging myself!

LET ME REMEMBER THAT MY GOAL IS GOD

I pick up my Workbook and feel guided to take another look at yesterday's lesson. I went out last night to a friend's place for a barbecue. I was quite tired, and knowing I wasn't in the headspace to continue with my lesson, I placed it aside. A feeling tells me that it is okay to redo a lesson if it feels right. It has been almost a year to date since commencing the lessons, and I am now at lesson number 258. However, I do recall it being recommended in ACIM that we do only one lesson at a time. So I do make sure that I focus on one lesson at a time before moving on to the next. It is interesting how the lesson I had difficulty with yesterday is **Lesson 258. Let me remember that my goal is God.** [WB, pg 423] Looking back at yesterday, I suppose that God wasn't my goal. Hmm, quite an important message there. So today, I will make it my goal to remember my lesson and remember God. I read on to the first paragraph. **All that is needful is to train our minds to overlook all little senseless aims, and to remember that our goal is God. His memory is hidden in our minds, obscured but by our pointless little goals which offer nothing, and do not exist.** As I read this the thought of "separation" comes to my mind, and I question why do we, as a separated ego, look to fill ourselves with goals in this world?

This feeling emerges that says, "All of the earthly desires can't fill that void you feel within. As soon as you make earthly goals more important than the goal of God, you jump on that hamster wheel and you keep spinning the wheel until you realize this is enough. You think there must be something more. And there is something more, that 'something more' is the memory of God."

I turn to my lesson and read on. **Shall we continue to allow God's grace to shine in unawareness, while the toys and trinkets of the world are sought instead? God is our only goal, our only love. We have no aim but to remember Him.** [WB, pg 423, 1.3] I must realize that happiness and peace will not be found in this dream. I look "out there" and think I will find what I need. My senses tell me I will find all that will make me happy in this world. However, I must know that those senses are coming from the voice of fear. This voice tells me all I ever need will be given unto me. It tells me that I need look no further than this large world of wonderful toys and trinkets. Hmm, at times there seems to be a fine line between the Voice of Love and the voice of fear. Once again, the good news is I am becoming more aware every day of the ego's tricks to delay me and keep me running on that hamster wheel! I pause to repeat my lesson, **Let me remember that my goal is God.** Yes, my goal is God. I take a moment to feel God's presence. I feel Love within me, next to me, above me, and below me. I feel the presence of God everywhere. It feels really good. Today is the day I will remember my goal is God.

FILLING THAT VOID

I have been spending some time journaling and relaxing in paradise today. I love to journal. I always feel connected with Holy Spirit and receive many messages each time I journal.

Earlier today a friend stopped over. This friend was crying and distraught. She had spent last night with her ex-boyfriend, only to learn earlier this morning that he has been seeing another woman. As I comfort her, I recognize that this character portrayed by her ex-boyfriend is truly just another trinket of this world. A character that is a representation of the egoic mind that offers her a replacement of the goal for God. How can this possibly make her happy?

She stopped sobbing for a moment to say, "I don't understand. Why do I keep going back to him when all I get from him is pain?" I tell her that the reason she continually returns to him is that he is filling a void for her. She asked me what else can fill that void. I paused and thought about it. And I replied, "Your own self-love is what will fill that void." I felt guided to tell her that. I am not so sure that she would be ready to hear that God would fill that void. Besides, where God resides within us is also where the Sonship resides. And I feel that an earthly understanding that helps us to relate to the "Truth" within is identifying with our own "self-love" within.

Between her tears, she said, "But I want to be held. I want to be touched. I want to be loved. Why can't this man love me like I want him to?" I pause for a moment, and then tell her, "He is unable to love you like you want him to because he also has voids, and if he can't love himself then how can he possibly give you the love that you desire?" She looked up at me and said, "You know what, that makes a lot of sense, it really does."

I explained to her that she can try to fill the void within by many things, like relationships, food, drugs, alcohol, etc. It's all the same, an "outer experience" giving a false sense of fulfillment. I told her I had been through similar experiences over the years and had come to realize that nothing out there could make me continually, truly happy. However, unfortunately, we have to know what we don't want to turn around and ask for what we do want. Or, we must walk through the darkness to get to the Light. It seems a cruel way to learn, I think to myself.

I look back over my life as I listened to her and realize this is not a sane world. I have read that in the Course, but it is now sinking in. ACIM makes more sense every day. Yes, there are times when we have utter enjoyment, but there are many times when we have pain too. And for the most part we walk blindly and we walk lost in this unknowing world. And why? Because we still haven't figured out that *true* Love is the *only* way to fill that ongoing void.

I looked into her eyes and said, "I promise you, sweetie, that this relationship will never fill the void that you are craving to fill. It can't. Journal, write, and speak to your Inner Self. Ask for guidance. And you will be guided toward what will make you feel good." I then asked her if she recognized the guidance she has within. And she said, "Oh yeah, you mean like when I had a gut feeling that he was seeing someone else? And when things didn't add up? And I just knew something was wrong?" I said, "Yes, okay, great. So, now, Journal and speak to *that* part of you. It is with you all the way. It is *your* Higher Self within. It is always trying to guide you through feelings. But we all think we are on our own, and so we don't listen to that guidance. We ignore it. We are usually not so aware when we are even receiving it because we get caught up in our own thinking and control. But if you get to know this other part of you then you will get to know the *true you.*"

IDENTIFYING MY RELATIONSHIPS WITH THE COURSE

I love Hawaii-Kai. I have been nestled here in my friend's backyard for the last 10 minutes watching fish jump out of the waterway. I see the fish jump here often. The hills in the background are so pretty on this June morning. They are gently stroked with soft oranges, reflecting the rising sun, and offset from the picturesque forefront of palms, houses, and waterways. Hmm, no matter how beautiful this is, I can enjoy it, but in the back of my mind I am softly reminded that I haven't woken up yet...this is still the illusion. Bummer, I thought someone else had found that light switch! Another gentle reminder follows that tells me, "This doesn't compare to what lies ahead, Robyn...when you finally do wake up!"

As the day passes, I find this is a day that I am able to remember my lesson. I am staying more connected today, and it seems that Holy Spirit is able to reach me to remind me. I have also come to realize that when I see my surroundings for what they are, and that is illusionary and not real, then it seems to assist me in staying connected on an ongoing basis.

As I climb into bed my thoughts wander to Ian. My relationship with Ian seems to get closer, and more connected, daily. Lately, I have been working at seeing him as the Son of God, and it does help a lot. We just skyped each other. To touch him right now would be worth all the gold in the Islands. And to feel his hand on my cheek would be worth every plane ticket back to the mainland. I know this is the ego part of me that yearns for this; however, I also know that it's okay. I do feel that I can enjoy my relationship with Ian and just remember in the back of my mind what the truth really is. Well, I am starting to get tired so I think it is time to turn off the light and dream another dream for now.

I lay in bed, about to turn off the light, and I feel a desire rise from within to pick up the pen. I have been thinking about my romantic relationship and the desire we have for each other. Can I make this relationship important and still plan to go home? Is that possible? I can feel that we are meant to be together. The feelings I have for Ian are very strong and we connect in so many different ways. So, can I enjoy this relationship at the level I wish and still go home?

This feeling comes over me that tells me I can enjoy my relationship with Ian but I just can't make the relationship more important than going home. I also get this feeling that we will grow closer in a different type of love as judgment ceases and forgiveness sets in. I just have to learn to trust in "going home." At times, like in my relationship, I feel as though I am going to have to give up something in order to go home. It does feel that way. And I guess in actual fact it is true. But it feels like I must give up something to get nothing. What do I get in return? If only I could know. From the small glimpse I have had, I feel like the Love will be powerful and never ending. I get that much. And I know it will feel good. But something deep down inside of me is still scared. Scared that if I actually do complete my forgiveness lessons and release the ego, and say goodbye to this world, then will I want it back? Will I miss something that I have with Ian? Will I want the bodily containment back, with all its senses? I think of touch, and how much I love to feel Ian's touch and how I love to touch him. Will there be something as wonderful as that when I go home? Wow, I keep forgetting that this is not real. I seem to remember the Truth slightly and then forget again and trip myself up with this type of questioning.

So then, who is making all of this real? The ego part of me of course. Because if I make it all real then I will be afraid to go home! Well, I guess if I do my forgiveness lessons within my relationship with Ian, then all that can happen to the relationship is positive, right? All that can happen is good. It can't be bad. Ego aspects will leave the relationship. So, the relationship can only get better. I guess at the end of the day I have to ask myself, "Do I want to feel good or do I want to feel bad?" Of course I want to feel good. And I believe in *A Course in Miracles.* I believe in Jesus' teachings about forgiveness. It makes so much sense to dissipate the ego. A feeling right now is telling me. "Isn't that all you need to know, Robyn? Do the work, because you know it will make your relationship better, and all of your other relationships better. You won't look back, Robyn. There will be nothing to look back at, except for dissipation of unwanted ego. You will look back at ego and you will be glad that it is behind you."

Ah, that feels better. My fear always seems to get the better of me until I can relax and allow Holy Spirit back in. I love it when I receive answers from Holy Spirit. When I begin to throw the questions out there the answers are never too far away! Okay, now I think I feel ready for a good night's sleep. Ni-night.

Chapter 10

Preparing to Wake Up

THE TRUTH IS ALWAYS REVEALING ITSELF

I am sitting on Lanikai beach this morning working on my lesson, and I turn to read page 419, **4. What is sin?** (the page I must read prior to each lesson in this section), when all of a sudden this message surfaces from within...

"Why does the Son need 'senses' when he has everything he already needs? He *is* pure, powerful Love. The sinner, the ego, needs senses, as it is useless without them. They give it a level of existence, and of hope. You don't need them, Robyn. You have a greater 'knowing.' It is all 'who you are naturally.' You can know everything in the blink of an eye when you are paying attention. All is revealed to you, because you are a powerful source of never ending Love that bears ALL knowledge."

Wow, I wasn't expecting that! Sometimes, when I receive a message it can really surprise me when I wasn't asking a relative question in that moment. I suppose in having to read this same page (page 419) each day prior to lessons 251-260, shows me that it is a very important message—just one that I wasn't paying enough attention toward. Hmm, I think I will take a break from my lesson and go jump in the water for a while to digest what I just heard.

Okay, that feels better. The water is just beautiful here at this beach. It always looks so inviting. I don't think I have seen water this color before. It is the most brilliant light blue. Now I feel refreshed and ready to get back into my lesson. That was quite an interesting message I received earlier. I love it when messages come through like that—when I am not questioning or looking for an answer in the moment, and Holy Spirit comes right on in like he never left the conversation yesterday!

I guess as far as senses go, I need to keep reminding myself that all *pure* answers come from the *Truth* in the form of feelings from *within*—not in the form of bodily senses. I think of my senses—smelling, seeing, hearing, taste, and touch— being functional attributes of the body. However, understanding that I must begin to ignore these bodily senses and deem them unnecessary all of a sudden is quite difficult to do. Well, for now, at least Holy Spirit has brought to my awareness the importance of recognizing that *all* answers are available through another source, our Spiritual source, or in other words, our Truth, rather than our illusionary source, the body.

I CAN'T HAVE BOTH

As I sit here in silence I can remove my attention from my surroundings and then feel that God exists here. He is not some place far away. He is right here, and He is everywhere.

My feelings tell me the memory of God will return fully when I do wake up from this dream. It still feels scary to dismantle this dream. But I was just given another glimpse of the Love that surrounds me—the Love of God. It feels blissful, free, gentle, accepting, and all-loving.

Just now as I write this, I realize in the following instant that I can't have BOTH. I truly can't have both! I can't have this dream *and* the pure Presence of God. As soon as I look at the dream and make it real, I lose sight of God. But when I choose to release the dream from my awareness and place my focus on God, the difference is amazing! I still place so much importance on the dream. But I realize I can't have both. If I continue to choose the dream and make the dream real, then I can't have God in my vision also. I can only have one, either God or the dream.

JOINING TO ASSIST

A friend called this afternoon that needed an ear. I listened to her and gave some support. However, I found myself getting caught up in her problem and making it real. Her expressions and concerns about her problem just made it seem so real and not illusionary at all. But then, she has no idea that this is a dream. And I wasn't about to blurt it out to her that it is one. So, when this happens, how do I help another without getting caught up in the dream with them? While I make it real, along with them, then I am staying stuck in the dream. So, what is the answer? It is not easy, and maybe not even the right answer, to just say to someone. "Oh, forget about it, this is just a dream, it's not real. What he did to you or what he said to you isn't real anyway." I mean some people aren't ready to hear that. So I am finding myself at a crossroad in between "wanting to wake up and wanting to help my brother feel better."

So, this friend called again just now—an hour later. As she was beginning to give me further explicit details of her problem, I felt an urge from within to stop her and let her know that peace can't come from focusing on the past. Peace comes from focusing on the present. She stopped and seemed to understand. Though, after a few seconds passed, she continued to tell me about her problem. Again, I received the same urge. I told her that this happened yesterday, and if she wanted to repeat the problem, then focusing on yesterday's problem would offer that. Then I got this feeling to see the Sonship in her and not the egoic problem. In the next moment I realized that if she is me then this is *my* problem too. I saw the problem as illusionary and decided not to make it real. I told her that if I were her I would choose *Love* instead of the problem. That was all I said, and she stopped and said, "Oh, you are so right! If I focus on my problem, things will only get worse. But if I choose Love instead of my problem, then things can only get better!

Wow. That wasn't so difficult after all. It felt really good to see her as the Sonship, rather than getting caught up in the egoic problems within the dream. And I actually didn't need to bring up the dream at all! All I needed to do was choose to see the Sonship in her and join with that. And then let the messages come through that I could share with her!

FALLING BACKWARDS

Ian and I had an argument last night. Now, today I feel awful, and I know he does too. I wish we could have peace all the time. I don't like it when the ego takes over in our relationship. When love is dominant, we have such a nice time together, but when the ego surfaces it changes everything. I don't want to walk away and complain as I know that will only attract more of the same, yet I get upset with myself for not handling it any better at the time.

This feeling comes to me that says, "Robyn, you have to know that this is part of the journey and you have to forgive yourself for getting upset and angry. It's okay that you get upset; it is giving you acknowledgment of the problem. You must learn to be patient with yourself while you 'unlearn' here. When you walk down this path and *decide* to release the ego then wrong-minded thoughts will surface so you can forgive them. As you continue to remind yourself this is all part of a dream then the easier this will all become. The ego knows how to control and get what it wants. It wants 'separation.' When you and Ian butt heads, then you want to blame him and he wants to blame you. That keeps you separate. To join with him, you have to forgive him for what you *thought he did wrong.* It is not always easy to do a forgiveness lesson *in the moment* while the ego is running around the hamster wheel. But as soon as you refocus and reconnect then you can do a forgiveness lesson. And in time, as you gain a greater understanding of forgiveness lessons, you will be able to do them in the moment. Be patient with yourself. With the right focus and work it WILL happen in time and at the right time. So enjoy the journey, be easy on yourself, and remember your brother is *you!*"

FEELING NO CONTAINMENT

This morning, I consider my lesson and the thought of being as God created me. **Lesson 260. Let me remember God created me.** [WB, pg 424] As I focus on this thought and stay with it, I soon feel no containment. I feel that my entity continues on forever, or in other words, the *true* me continues on forever, and nothing is in the way of extending my love. That is always a good start for me. Feeling no containment helps me to feel the freedom of who I truly am. I feel no control, no anxiety, and no guilt. All I feel is absolute freedom. It sure feels good. Just imagine, God created this? No terror, no anxiety, no guilt, and certainly no judgment. Wow, I stop to enjoy His presence.

It feels protective and all-knowing. I feel like a child, and God is saying, "This way. Come this way. Don't go back there. Don't slumber anymore. I want you here with me. I created you in my image as my companion and fellow creator. Cease indentifying yourself falsely. It is time to wake up and remember your Truth!"

After completing my lesson a number of times today, I feel really great. My lesson has helped me to see that judgment, guilt, anxiety, and control is all here in this dream. The open, vulnerable, loving, all-encompassing purity of every good feeling we can imagine was shown to me today. I've had glimpses before, but today, through my lesson, I have been shown more. It was like a complete knowing was present, with nothing missing.

Sometimes I wonder how a spiritual love that we can't see can actually be real. But then to stay in that moment and feel that glimpse of purity, as I did earlier, feels so real. It didn't feel fake or false at all. To feel wholly accepted feels light years away from the understanding I have developed about myself within this dream. I know now that if I want to experience more of that freedom, and more of that ongoing pure state of bliss, then I must forge ahead. I must continue to learn how to undo the ego. Not glorify it and make it special. From now on, I want to see the Truth in others. I want to see them as the Sonship. I want to not only see them as my brother; I truly want to see them as myself!

What I would like to know is if it does get this good, then why did we ever choose the ego existence? Why did we dream a dream where terror, judgment, control, and anxiety exist? Why? The feeling I am getting is that we will know later. We only need to learn how to wake up for now. We don't need to know why or how we fell asleep.

I have decided that I want to wake up and taste that wonderful feeling forever! Hey, I wonder if there are other Sons that God created? Or, I wonder if we are able to create our own Sonship? This feeling tells me not to get ahead of myself and just take all this one day at a time.

As I look out over the water, I still crinkle my nose at the thought of this being some random, crazy dream. The feeling of the energy within the dream seems to be a low, dense, foggy type of energy. My mind shifts from the dream as I repeat my lesson for the day, **Let me remember God created me.** Okay, that feels better. Thinking about God being my Father and me being an essence of pure Love in His image is better than focusing on the dream!

The birds are singing away in the trees across the waterway. I just watched a fish do multiple jumps in a row. I tried to picture him under the water taking a run for the surface. Then he flies through the air, and plops back in, only to propel himself toward the surface again. I know I am easily amused. But then this dream is quite amusing don't you think? I mean what were we thinking? We created a fish that jumps out of the water for pleasure. We created these odd looking venomous centipedes that you find on this island. They are huge. I saw one the other day that was about 7 inches long. Damn, that thing looked creepy. So, why did we bring a venomous centipede along for this crazy ride? Part of this dream is happy and part of this dream is scary. Were we trying to mimic God's creation of love in a way? And then we got lost in it all and fell into fear?

My Inner Voice is saying, "Does it really matter?" No, but if it's not real, then why doesn't it just disappear? There are poisonous animals that attack, fires that burn, and cyclones that destroy. Not to mention the earthquakes, which I have had the pleasure of experiencing. We seem to spend part of our time in wonder and happiness and then part of our time in pain and anxiety. When I consider yesterday, the whole day sure seems like a dream right now. It's all just a memory...and how real are memories? That always helps when I think about that. So, how many people out there think this is some crazy dream? Really, how many in this world? I think I met one once in Oz. He walked, talked, and acted just like I would have expected Jesus to if he walked in my front door. I remember being amazed by his presence one night as I cooked him and a friend dinner. If that guy wasn't enlightened he must have been close to it. I've often wondered about him. He was such a gentle soul. I wonder if *he* knew this was a dream.

Well, I guess I have to look beyond the beauty of the birds singing, the fish jumping, the tide flowing, and continue to tell myself it's just a dream. It's just a dream. It's just a dream. It's just a dream.

QUESTIONING ROMANTIC RELATIONSHIPS

Earlier I was talking to Ian about the ego and I came to realize that the ego can't survive on love alone. It needs the drama still. It needs the duality. It needs "separation" to survive. As I mulled over these thoughts, it became clear to me that when we no longer wish to live in duality, and we no longer wish to live in separation, then we have to decide, as *the* ego, that we don't want to be an ego anymore. When we come to that realization, then we, as the ego, have to make the decision, as Ian says, to issue the "silver bullet." Now, that has to be the most difficult decision that any of us are going to make in a lifetime! We are so attached to this dream and to everything in it. So, how do we get strong enough to give the ego, meaning the self that we know today, the silver bullet?

This morning I had a breakdown. I was in tears and was upset that everything was not as I had perceived all these years. For as long as I could remember, I wanted a romantic, blissful relationship. I used to think if only I could find that one person that will make me feel good, that will love me, adore me, and want the best for me. Today is a major turning point in my life as I realize for the first time that this is not the answer for feeling that ultimate kind of love. Who wanted this kind of love anyway? My ego wanted it. I realize today, through tears, that this blissful, romantic, passionate love also comes with duality. It cannot survive on *love* alone. It is a trap. Just another one of the ego traps. And it is a BIG one, because that is what so many of us desire to have throughout their lifetime. We desire a blissful, romantic, loving relationship; or as the Course calls it, a "special relationship." It is the one thing that we think will reveal the ultimate walk, the ultimate love...something like a piece of heaven.

I pause to consider what has dawned on me this morning. A romantic relationship appears to be the closest thing to heaven that the ego can experience. To me, it is by far the best part of the egoic dream. It doesn't get much better than being "in-love" in the dream. And then reality sets in as the ego can't live on that existence alone. What happened to duality? So, along comes the drama. While we expect this type of love to exist in our lives, then we have to take the bad with the good. Because the ego desires this type of love affair and the ego must have duality within the love affair to survive.

So then I take a step back. Ian takes a step back. Coming to the realization that what I wanted all these years is just a false part of this dream is heartbreaking. We both wanted this type of love for a very long time. So, I told Ian, through my tears, what we always wanted was just another egoic desire to keep the dream alive. At first he didn't want to hear this either. But then he said he realized how the ego was very present in our relationship and we had to accept that. I explained to him about the duality of the ego. He understood, and then he asked me. "What happens when we forgive the ego and the ego dissipates? What type of love is left? Will we still love each other as deeply as we do in the dream?" I told him, "I don't know. I wish I could tell you. But I can tell you this much—my feelings tell me that once I begin to truly forgive the ego and move forward, then part of my ego falls away and I will see you with more loving eyes. There won't appear to be as much negative stuff going on. I would have forgiven it; therefore I would have released it. I do feel in my heart that there is a better love that we will witness. But in order to receive it, I must give up the attachment I have toward this other type of egoic love. While I am still giving so much importance to that blissful, romantic love, I will not find the *true* Love that resides in both you and me. It doesn't mean we can't enjoy the journey; all it does mean is when we choose to go home it can no longer be about the ego's needs and wants.

Yet again, I have reached another fork in the road where I stop to hand over the steering wheel. As I give up the ego's desire for "special love," and as Ian questions, "What *will* we have left?"...I can only offer the answer that my feelings provide me with. And that helps some right now, but it still feels like an awful lot to risk, especially when the romance is fresh for us. I can sit here and say that I hope to be in Ian's arms throughout this, and at the end of all this. This feeling from within tells me to have faith that all will unfold perfectly. I sit back and take a deep breath. Ok, I will try to find some faith here. It does feel that I am giving up an awful lot though, and I don't know how I'm going to do it. I suppose in recalling the times when I have followed my Inner Voice in the past, and it never disappointed me, does offer me a platform to build some faith on for now.

IS THERE A RIGHT WAY TO DO FORGIVENESS LESSONS?

Holy Spirit, how do I go about my forgiveness lessons the right way? When Ian and I get upset at each other, how do I release judgment? If I point the finger at him, I hurt him and then just attract more upset. Holy Spirit, how do I forgive correctly?

LATER THAT DAY

Sometimes I ask questions and don't receive the answer straight away; however, the answer does come at some point. I might receive it in the next hour or sometimes even the next day. I actually did learn in PF1 when I am not receiving an answer immediately it is because of my own disconnected state. Holy Spirit is *always* there. However, I am not always ready or willing to listen. So, this afternoon, when I was driving, this feeling comes to me that says, "Robyn, if you truly want to forgive Ian for anything you think he did wrong, then firstly, you have to see him as yourself, or in other words, as the Sonship. You wouldn't point the finger at yourself right? You would want to know you were innocent right? Well, when you see Ian as yourself, then you won't be as ready to point the finger. He truly is *you.*"

Following that, another feeling surfaces that says, "When you remember this is not your reality, then you will understand that what you thought he did never really happened. It was false. It was all part of a dream. You prefer him to feel good rather than bad, right?" Well, just know that the reason you want him to feel good is that at some level you still remember that he is *you.* It's only when you are angry and you separate from him that you want him to feel bad. As you continue to forgive the wrong mind, by seeing Ian as "you" and recognizing that it is only a dream, the easier it will be to stay connected and "choose Love" Instead of the wrong-minded thought. Just remember, you are in this together to help each other out of the dream. The way out of the dream is to see the ego and then forgive it—which is the only way to dissipate it. Each time you witness something that you are wishing to forgive, call on Me to assist, and I will reveal the Truth to you. I will stand with you and show you the way. You and Ian have come together to help each other, just like your lesson today, under the Theme of Special Relevance, number **5. What is the body?** [WB, pg 425, 4.3] **The Son of God extends his hand to**

reach his brother, and to help him walk along the road with him. Now is the body holy. Now it serves to heal the mind that it was made to kill. Robyn, you are helping your brother come home. Your relationship *is* about helping each other return home. Stay focused on that, enjoy each other's company along the way, and you will arrive at your destination."

MAXIMIZING THE TRUTH

I realize today that going home must be the most important thing to me—more important than anything. I feel that Ian is definitely important to me. I feel a lot of love for him. However, I can't make my relationship with him more important than going home. I can tell at times that me doing this work scares him. He wants to undo the ego, and he has known that for years. But when I tell him how important it is for me to go home, I understand why he feels like I am minimizing our relationship. I guess in a way he is right? As I consider this thought, a feeling surfaces that tells me, "Robyn, the ego invented the 'special' romantic relationship. Now you can make it a 'holy relationship' and use it as your means to go home. Yes, you minimize the importance of the 'special' relationship but you maximize the importance of Ian's Truth. You are maximizing your knowledge and understanding of the Sonship in him!"

I sit in silence digesting what I have just heard when another feeling surfaces from within that says, "Robyn, if you want to heal and go home then you must be willing to forgive your brother and forgive yourself. No-one is to blame. Nobody did anything to anyone. It is all part of *your* dream."

Chapter 11

My Holy Vision

CAN I SEE MY BROTHER AS MYSELF?

It is a beautiful day out there in paradise. I just arrived back from shopping. The post office was unusually busy this morning. There was a long line of waiting customers, including a few unhappy ones. I heard one woman complaining to the customer service officer that they should have more staff attending the front counter. As I listened to her, I quickly recalled my lesson for the day, **lesson 262. Let me perceive no differences today.** [WB, pg 426] This feeling came over me that said, "Robyn, you are one with this person. This problem is an error that is in *your* mind. See it as *your* problem too and forgive it." Following that, a vision came to me that showed the egoic mind as a big pot of stew, just stewing away. We each take portions from this stew of wrong-minded information. And we all own this one big pot because we are one. So, if I am witnessing this incident in the post office then it is an error in my mind also. The answer is to see the wrong-minded thought as illusionary, forgive it, and join with my brother. Problems come from fear and will separate us. Seeing the problem as illusionary comes from love and will join us.

As I enter the backyard and look toward the glistening waters, I consider this big ego pot and all the information it must hold. I take a seat on the sun lounge and pick up my lesson. I repeat, **Let me perceive no differences today.** My thoughts begin to wander, and I find them tuning into a straggly looking guy that had walked by me in Waikiki yesterday. As this man walked into my vision, I had pulled back in my seat while holding my lesson tightly, hoping that he wouldn't come any closer and bother me. Then I looked at my lesson, it was lesson 262. Yes, I am redoing it today. I had a head-ache last night, and didn't do it all evening. Meanwhile, my Inner Voice is telling me not to make excuses, and it's ok if I didn't finish my lesson and it's fine I am redoing it today. Ok, so back to the straggly guy. I felt edgy as he walked closer to where I was sitting. Then I realized that he was stumbling as he walked, and was just stumbling my way. He straightened up some, clasped his red duffle bag and bright green umbrella (which looked like he'd found in a nearby trash can) then he was on his way. I relaxed and continued with my lesson. As I read my lesson, this passage got my attention... *Why should I perceive a thousand forms in what remains as one? Why should I give this one a thousand names, when only one suffices? For Your Son must bear Your Name, for You created him. Let me not see him as a stranger to his Father, nor as stranger to myself.* [WB, pg 426, 1.4] As I read this, I realized I was just offered an opportunity to join with my brother. At first I felt like a bad Course student. Then I realized that at least I got it. What a great time to be revising my lesson! I might have passed by the opportunity if it was any other time of the day. I decided to join with the straggly guy. Oh...I mean my brother. I pictured in my mind that we are one. Then I said to myself, "Could it be true? This man is me?" I considered it some more and then felt through to his Spirit where we join. I felt the connection. I felt myself.

As my mind comes back to this moment in Hawaii-Kai, I look at my surroundings and the lovely homes that line the water's edge. I wonder why we choose the path that we choose? Is it just that some of us appear more lost in finding our way home than others? And this guy, my brother, did he choose this path for his own reasons? I ponder the questions. This feeling tells me that we are all in this together, and the choice is ours to support and help each other along the way. As I write this, I recall the section on page 425 of the Workbook. **The Son of God extends his hand to reach his brother and to help him walk along the road with him. Now is the body holy. Now it serves to heal the mind that it was made to kill.** [WB, pg 425, 4.3] Hmm, we each extend our hands to our brother to help him walk along the road. I thought of how much a smile could have made a difference to that guy's day yesterday. Right then my fear came back as I found myself saying, "But what if he came and sat next to me?" Wow, I stopped myself. That means I am scared of my brother! Why am I scared I wonder? I guess it is because I have been conditioned to be scared of people like him. In my mind, I decided to replay the scenario, and brought him back to where he was with his bright green umbrella and red duffle bag. Once I got past my egoic judgment, I managed to see through to his Truth. And it felt good. I felt the connection as I saw him as my brother, and self. I then sent him some loving energy as he stumbled by.

So now I ask Holy Spirit to assist me in remembering that each soul is my brother today. Please help me to see beyond the egoic wrong mind Holy Spirit and join in oneness with all my brothers!

ROMANCE IS IN THE AIR

Yesterday, I moved into a small unit in Lanikai for the month of July. It is one block from the beach. With Ian coming into town I figured that it would be nice to have our own little beach pad. So, today is the day that Ian arrives. Woohoo! Today is July 3rd, and so he will be arriving just in time for July 4th celebrations. I am about to head to the florist to get him a lei and then pick him up at Honolulu airport. I haven't seen him, well live, for about a month. I am so excited to hold him and touch him again!

As I head to the airport, I wonder how my personal journey will affect our relationship. I mean, after all, I am quite serious about the Course now, and he is quite happy to enjoy this dream and keep moseying along. Which is fine with me. I am just wondering how it will affect our relationship. And if it is possible for us to continue enjoying each other while I plan on going home and he plans on staying. Will we see eye to eye along the way? This feeling comes to me that says, "Robyn, Robyn, Robyn, just let it all go and enjoy the journey. It is okay that you have different ideas about the dream today. All is okay, just keep doing what feels good, and if this feels good, then it must be good!"

Meeting Ian at the airport was a lot of fun. I slipped the lei around his neck and we kissed and hugged like a couple of childhood sweethearts that hadn't seen each other for years. We were both so happy to be together again. We left the airport, bound for Lanikai, both of us beaming with excitement for a huge week of aloha fun that lay ahead!

A FEW DAYS LATER

Ian and I have been having so much fun here on the East Coast of Oahu. The day he arrived, we hung out on Lanikai Beach, soaked up the sun, the water, and each other of course, and just really relaxed. It was so nice to be together again! The first night, we found our favorite restaurant on Oahu, called Buzz's. Buzz's is in Kailua, which is the town next to Lanikai. We found the name interesting as my father's nickname was Buzz, the publishing company for my first book was called Buzzworld, and one of Ian's good buddies is called Buzz. We were seated at the presidents table (where Bill and Hillary Clinton once sat) under this beautiful painting which we both admired very much. Then, funny enough, the following day, just by sheer coincidence, we were introduced by a friend to a local artist called Michael. As we chatted, Michael mentioned that one of his paintings was hung above the presidents table at Buzz's. We told him that we had sat at that very table admiring his work the previous evening! He had two prints remaining out of 10 that were for sale, so we visited his home in Lanikai and Ian happily bought one. The picture shares an array of brilliant oranges and blues, depicting a warm, early evening on the shoreline of Lanikai Beach. It is really a beautiful piece.

The next day was July 4th. That evening we decided to check out the local fireworks show. We found an ideal location sitting upon a bluff overlooking Kailua Bay. It was the perfect romantic spot. The fireworks showered the sky overhead and then sprinkled across the bay below us. Later we also had our own fireworks display back at the house where we were staying. It was all great fun.

Yesterday we swam with honu's (Hawaiian for turtles). We found a few swimming around the bay at Kailua. We swam alongside them and took photos. I don't know if they were hunting for food at that time of the day but they seemed to be on a mission and were actually swimming very fast. It became quite a workout to catch up with one and then swim alongside it. Ian and I have a great time together, and yes, it does make me want things to be like this forever! These times are definitely a cool part of the dream.

I have been continuing with my lessons while Ian is here, and he is supportive in me doing them, which is great. He understands that I want to spend time on them and he has been very good about it. The only thing I have found, with Ian here, is that my focus isn't as strong as it needs to be. Which, I suppose makes sense after all that time apart. It has been exciting to have him here and thoughts of him have been occupying my mind quite a bit. So, I have been feeling the need to repeat my lessons. How unusual! However, as long as I do them to the best of my ability, then I must just move forward knowing that all is unfolding perfectly.

QUESTIONING MY BROTHER'S ACTIONS

Sometimes it is difficult to see a brother as myself, especially when I feel I have been unfairly treated. For instance, when I rented this unit in Lanikai for the month of July, I was looking for a small place near the beach where Ian and I could relax, and also a quiet place where I could write. The owner is a lady who rents out this place as a vacation unit. It is attached to her beautiful home on the hillside of Lanikai. When I initially called the lady, I told her I would spend some time writing in Lanikai, and ideally would like something with a nice lanai and a quiet spot to write. She offered me a garden view unit that she had available. I asked her if I could take a look at it the following week when I would be in Oahu. She explained that I wouldn't be able to see the unit as she was leaving for the mainland the next day. She also said the unit would work well for me and would suit my requirements; however, if I didn't make the decision straight away, I could lose it. She then asked me to send the full payment.

I didn't want to lose the unit as there were not many available in Lanikai, so I trusted her and sent the money. It turns out the lanai is extremely small. It's about half the size of the photo that I had seen on the internet. Plus the house, though in a quaint, quiet town like Lanikai, is situated on a busy road and the cars make a ton of noise all day long. I never would have dreamed Lanikai could be this noisy. The reason I chose this area to write is because I thought all of Lanikai would be peaceful. How could it be noisy when there is not one single shop, and only one road that loops around something like a mile radius of residential homes nestled at the base of a foothill? Oh, except, for the beach, which, by the way, is classed as one of the top 10 beaches in the world. Hmm, so, I guess that right there might have something to do with all this traffic! Did I mention I was blonde?

Anyway, the chance of it being noisy was something I never considered. Plus, I would have thought the lady would have known this situation would not be a good one for a writer. Granted, the unit is very nice inside and has all I need, but I wouldn't have taken the unit if I had visited it prior to paying. So today, as I do my lesson, **Lesson 263. My Holy vision sees all things as pure,** [WB, pg 427] I feel I am tested to see her as holy. Actually, when I first arrived, and realized these things, I saw her as anything but holy. So today, I have been asking myself who's judging this? Of course, my wrong mind, or the ego, is judging this. So, if I want to remove the ego, how can it be removed when I am coming from wrong mind and giving this so much attention?

I feel guided to recall **Lesson 16. I have no Neutral thoughts.** [WB, pg 26] I read on to paragraph 1.2. **Everything you see is the result of your thoughts. There is no exception to this fact. Thoughts are not big or little; powerful or weak. They are merely true or false. Those that are true create their own likeness. Those that are false make theirs.**

When something happens unexpectedly it is not always so easy to stop ourselves and say, "Ok, I am projecting this." When this happened, I did stop myself and knew that my thoughts were not forgiving. But not long after, I found myself complaining about it again, and then I would catch myself again. I decided this morning, after doing my lesson, to put pen to paper and write about how I was feeling. As I began to write about my thoughts, this feeling came over me that said,

"Robyn, it is only a dream. And you are each playing out roles to assist each other with forgiveness lessons. You have an opportunity now to forgive. What will be your choice? Will your choice be to complain and remain as ego in this dream? Or, will your choice be to forgive then keep heading home?"

I got it, and thanked Holy Spirit. When I write it seems to free up my mind and then Holy Spirit can enter and help me to see the truth again.

Straight away another feeling followed that said, "Robyn, see it as false. See that it's not real. And beyond that, keep telling yourself that this woman is your brother. She is you! Know that she is playing out her part in this dream. And then, each time you do that, with every situation, it will get easier and easier to remember. The first question to ask yourself is: Do I want to stay stuck in this dream, or do I want to go home? When you finally get serious about going home, Robyn, is when you will remember right away that you must forgive. Do you want to stay stuck and keep coming back here, or do you want to go home to continual bliss, freedom, and peace?"

WHAT HAVE I GOT TO LOSE?

Today, Ian and I are going to the North Shore for some snorkeling and sunning. We both love the East Coast and the North Shore here on Oahu. It is all so beautiful. And we are enjoying it all as much as we can. I am going to miss Ian heaps when he leaves, that's for sure. But for now, it's "live in the moment" time!

Ian just left for a walk to get his morning coffee. I am sitting on my lanai enjoying the beautiful palms and lush tropical landscape. Each morning I collect the plumeria flowers that have fallen from the large plumeria tree which shades my lanai, and I spread them across the garden table and place one behind my ear. It is really a neat little spot. Since I arrived, I have come to overlook the noise problem and enjoy the beauty that exists here instead. I have grown quite fond of my little garden unit and lanai, and really enjoy being here, to the point where I would stay here again in the future! Looking back, once I got that message from Holy Spirit it helped me to feel much better. And I guess those forgiveness lessons have been working too! It all feels good.

Ian and I have many interesting conversations. Earlier this morning we were discussing PF1 and how much of it, if any, do we bring forward to assist in going home. As Ian and I were chatting, I explained to him how in PF1 I was in control of the dream through the process of visualizing. At that time, it felt as though I had both hands firmly on the steering wheel. I look back and realize I was in control of what I was receiving on a day to day basis, and I had gotten very good at it—controlling the dream that is.

When Holy Spirit initially asked me to hand over the steering wheel it wasn't so hard to do because I had also learned to have faith in the guidance I was receiving. This faith in guidance I had learned in PF1. As I handed over the steering wheel it was like I had to put PF1 on a shelf and allow Holy Spirit to show me what aspects of that knowledge were in line with the knowledge of the Course. It was as though I couldn't just go and join the two together. Now I can see why. The two vital steps I have been guided to bring forward are "understanding projection" and "faith in the Voice within." I once felt confused as to why I had been previously guided to spend so much time learning PF1 prior to PF2. But, now, as I look back, I can see how PF1 certainly assisted in staging my journey for a better understanding and participation of PF2.

Ian and I also talked about the difficulty in making the decision to terminate the ego. We talked about the possibility of dying young in this lifetime (upon waking up). That definitely brought up a lot of fear, and was something that initially bothered me with the Course. I do recall the one thing that helped me to feel better about making this seemingly brutal choice of terminating myself. When I looked at other teachers of the Course and saw how many of them still lived long lives while doing the Course, I then realized that the chances of me still living a long life would be high. I also realized that getting rid of this ego could end up being a lifetime's work! So, what have I got to lose? Just an ego really!

VISITING THE MOKULUA'S...AND GOD

This morning was such a pretty morning. The waters of Lanikai were still and peaceful, so Ian and I decided to kayak over to the Mokulua's, which are the twin islands off the coastline of Lanikai Beach. It took about 40 minutes to paddle there. The island on the left is said to resemble an ape walking through the water. It does look pretty cool, and from a distance looks as though huge shoulders and the head of an ape are surfacing out of the water. After arriving at this particular island, we decided to leave our kayaks and go for a hike along the rocky walls of the coastline. We were prepared with our reef shoes to assist in climbing around the rocks. As we climbed, Ian stopped to point out the lava tubes which curved their way down the face of these huge rocks. I followed him as he led us to a large rock pool, which we were pleased to find, and jumped in to cool ourselves off.

When we arrived back to the beach point of the island where our kayaks were, we decided to check out the seabed below and went for a snorkel. We were hoping to see more honu's, but there was barely even a fish to be found; most likely due to the plentiful kayaks that would visit this island on a daily basis I would imagine.

As we lay on the sand to soak up the warm rays and dry off, I pause to repeat my lesson. **Lesson 264. I am surrounded by the Love of God.** [WB, pg 427] In the quiet of the moment, I feel the Love that surrounds me. A memory begins to surface and I recall that time in meditation when I felt God's Love everywhere. I remember thinking, "Wow, what a beautiful feeling to feel the Love of God within everything!" Today, as I consider my lesson, I am beginning to understand this to a larger degree. I look around me and feel the presence of God's Love, and stay in that place for a moment, when suddenly I feel the presence of everything else disappear—the sand, the rocks, and the brilliant light blue ocean of Lanikai! I feel the presence of God's Love absolutely everywhere. I feel God's Love within Ian, within myself, within the sand, the water, and the rocks. As I feel the Love, it is almost like everything disappears. It's as though it really ISN'T THERE. It was never there! And the Love I feel in place of everything is exaggerated enormously. The love I feel for Ian's Truth is exaggerated tenfold. It feels very accepting, encompassing, and joining.

So, today I made a choice, via my lesson, to see God's Love. And then magically, in that moment, God's Love became all there was. But it also became the love of everything. If I could continue to do that, on an ongoing basis—if I could choose to see and feel God's Love—God's Love will become bigger, stronger, more dominant, and more real. As I repeat that, then that is more of what I will see and feel. The other stuff will disappear in time. And what I will be left holding is the vision of God's Love. It will become more dominant, more important, and more real. It all comes back to choice. What do I choose to see then? Do I choose to see the ego's work or do I choose to see God's work? So, that's what waking up really is! It is deciding to see God's Love and making it real instead of making the ego's work real! God's Love really does exist where all these other things exist, we just don't know it because we have made the ego's work so real. Wow, I thought I had begun to wake up. But now I can see that I haven't. While I still give

116

so much importance and meaning to everything around me and keep making it real, then I cannot for the life of me begin to see God, or the Sonship for that matter. I have to decide what I am going to see. I have to decide what really matters to me—Truth or the dream? When I finally choose Truth in each step is when the meaning of all else will fall away. It will disappear and carry no substance. And what will be left will be Truth. An unconditional, never ending Love, that resides within and around everything.

If I could remember to see God's Love in everything around me—the trees, the buildings, my brothers—then the more of God's Love is what I will see. If I could remember that all the time then how could I feel pain? How could I feel uncomfortable ever again?

A SENSE OF KNOWING

I'm a tad sad today. Ian left earlier to go back to the mainland. I wish he could stay and play here with me in paradise. But, unfortunately, California calls for Ian to return to work.

I have been considering God's Love everywhere these past few days as Ian and I hung out in this beautiful paradise together. I would stop and sense the Love everywhere and I could even share that with Ian, which was very cool. Ian has an open understanding about the Course and the journey I am on. I think we each have a respect for each other's outlooks and desires in life. I used to wonder, prior to meeting Ian, if I could in fact date a "non-Course" student. Now, I can honestly say that none of that matters. All that matters is understanding where I am today in my own life, and not questioning that.

As I look around me and envision God's Love everywhere, I feel a sense of safety and a sense of knowing. I can almost feel everything else disappear. I hold the thought and feel the Love get even larger. All of a sudden everything I have been studying within *A Course in Miracles* makes perfect sense. It really is all about Love! The dream is only real because I continue to see it as real. As long as I choose to make real what is around me then how can Love replace it? If I can make that choice in every step, then I will become more of who I truly am in every step. But how difficult is it to focus on Love in every step when all I see around me has appeared very real all my life? This feeling comes to me that says, "Robyn, this asking to *see* Truth has set your tone anew. You are becoming 'aware' of Love's presence everywhere—of God's presence everywhere. If you continue to desire more awareness of Love, then more awareness of Love will be yours."

I am taking in what I just heard when another feeling emerges that tells me, "You are not this body, Robyn. You are eternal Love. You will never die. Love doesn't die. As your lesson today suggests: **The body is the means by which God's Son returns to sanity.** [WB, pg 425, 4.1] Now is the time when you use the body as your vehicle, and as your means to go home. The ego will identify with fear of 'time' wherever it can. When lapse of time appears to be a detriment, the ego is only doing its job by alerting you to keep you here in the dream. You fear that if you release the egoic personality, that things will get worse and not better. Ian was right. It is the ego that fears that. That is because it is the end of the road for the ego. Do you truly want to go home? Are you sure? If you are sure and you know you want to go home, then go home you will. If you revert at any point and question yourself you will stay in the dream. Keep asking yourself what you choose and you will stay on the path that you choose. Also, keep asking yourself what is real, and what is real will continue to be revealed to you. It has to be. There is no way you can seek the Truth and not find it."

Chapter 12

Considering the Happy Dream

THE BEAUTY WITHIN THE DREAM

I've really enjoyed watching the sunsets these past couple of days. Heavy rain clouds sit on top of the high mountains behind Kailua and sprinkle yellow, pink, and oranges across the sky as the sun sinks behind. I am sitting on a small rock overlooking a little sandy beach laden with black volcanic rock. The mountains in the background look black right now. The sun setting looks magical against the black of the mountains, black rock, and deep blue sea in between. I grab my camera. I love photography. Though I never pursued photography, I have found much fun in it as a hobby, trying to capture moments of glory around this picturesque world that we dream. To think that the ego pieced this dream together is quite interesting. How can beauty come from fear? I guess it is just part of the happy dream. The part the ego creates that keeps us here. But then if the dream weren't somewhat happy, why would any of us consider staying at all and not seek some form of escape?

STUCK ON A LESSON

It is a new morning and I am sitting on my lanai in Lanikai soaking up the gorgeous Hawaiian sunshine as I complete my daily lesson. It seems to be a tad easier to get involved in each lesson when the sun is warming up every part of my body. This may come as no surprise, but I have been doing the same lesson for about a week now. Each day, I get a feeling to do the same lesson again. So I do. I actually thought I was giving some good attention to this lesson, but then I know at times I have strayed from it too. I suppose, as I look closely at this lesson, it does seem to encompass the whole of *A Course in Miracles*. **Lesson 264. I am surrounded by the Love of God.** [WB, pg 427]

I begin to feel my existence as the Son of God. Family, Ian and friends come into my mind as I consider the fact that we are not really who we think we are. I am truly not this body; neither is that guy jogging past the house right now.

As I feel my existence as the holy Son of God, I then feel my Truth. I look around me. None of this is real. I feel the Love that exists everywhere, and then everything else slowly loses validity. Everything becomes so unreal. All of a sudden this feeling sweeps my body that hasn't swept me before. This dream is uninteresting. What happens in this dream is false. Nothing has substance. It has nothing to offer me. I look at the cigarette I am holding (once in a while I have a cigarette, I know they fill a void, but, hey, it's a friend at times) and I suddenly conclude that at this level of truth, I don't need the cigarette. It does nothing for me. In fact, where I sit right now, on this different plain, I don't need anything!

I feel the "Oneness" with everything and with everyone. I realize I don't touch the steering wheel at all in this place. There is no need. There is nothing to control; no need to control anything. All of a sudden I see nothing ahead of me. I don't know the way, and it feels really good. I feel a connection to Higher Mind that gently wants my mind. It asks for my mind, my body, my eyes, my tongue, and my time. It wants to show me the way. It must be Holy Spirit. The connection between sanity and insanity it feels like. Something that says gently, "Relax and let go. I'll show you where to go and what to say. You don't need to feel concern. There is peace up ahead. Let go of everything."

It feels surreal, uncanny, large, and blissful to touch the Source that offers me pure guidance. I look around me and feel the emptiness of the dream. The dream has nothing to offer me from this place. I feel that nothing—not food, items, people, or anything in this dream can give me what I need. I can see the colored waters of Lanikai beach piercing through the trees in the distance. I see the beauty still but I feel that it has nothing to offer me.

Yesterday, as I watched the sun set behind the mountains, I watched an artist creating on his canvas to the right of me, while people were canoeing and fishing in the bay area beyond. As I watched everyone, I realized what all of us were doing. We were all looking for something to make us happy. And in the moment, when I looked around me, we were all doing something that was making us happy. Then, in the next instant, I realized that tomorrow most of us will feel some kind of frustration, sadness, or anger. So, this is, right now, in this moment, the happy part of the dream. But it dawned on me that we were all looking for something to make us happy. We all needed something to make us smile. To *need* is the greatest trait of the ego, in aid of keeping us here in this dream. We *need* to find something to fill that space within— that void. However, we don't know what will truly fill that void. We don't know what will truly make us happy. So, many of us keep looking. We find one thing that makes us happy for a while and then we look for another. It might be a hobby that fills the void for a while, or it might even be a relationship. There is always something else, something new around the corner, which can fill the void left behind from the last item or person that was in our life.

Understanding that everything is a need (absolutely everything in this dream that brings us some level of happiness is a need) helps me to finally see the disability of the ego. The ego has only one way to make better of this fearful entry into the dream. And that is to find some relief, some satisfaction, within the dream—to make it a happy dream.

Looking back, when I was deliberately manifesting in PF1, little did I know I was feeding my ego by making the dream happy all those years. There was nothing wrong with that of course. If we are not ready to exterminate the ego, then that is truly the next best thing—to shift our focus within the dream, and to help create a happier dream. It is doable. But it doesn't get around the *need* to fill the continual void that we feel within.

Neediness creates a continual battle for happiness within the dream. That is big. Finally coming to the realization that everything I derive happiness from in this dream is based on a need to fulfill my ego is truly a Godsend. I don't think I have felt this much understanding and relief from *A Course in Miracles* since I began the journey.

I look to my right. I am sitting on my lanai. My eyes rest upon this small statue of an owl sitting amongst the foliage. He seems to be looking straight at me. But he has no eyes. His eyes have weathered over time. I think of the reality of the dream—the only reality—and that is everything dissolves over time. Even my eyes will do the same thing. Need I wait till then to *see* from my Truth! Everything around me will dissolve. So what does that mean? The dream can't be eternal. So why wait? Happiness comes and goes in this dream. I want to feel that continual high—that continual bliss. And now I know I can. Now I know I must release what I "thought" would make me happy, to be shown what will truly make me happy! My focus goes to Ian instantly. I feel my ego surface at the thought of giving up control with the direction of this relationship. What if I don't have any say at all? What will I be guided toward? My Inner Guidance tells me to just relax and all will work out the way it is supposed to. Wow, releasing this is not so easy. But I recognize today that I am required to release *neediness* in all areas so I can be shown the Truth.

I look at everything I needed yesterday. I needed lots of friends, so I found lots of friends. I needed lots of recognition from these friends. In other words, I needed to be needed. I needed to be liked. But isn't that what the ego does? If it wasn't that, then it would have been something else. The ego plays out the role of neediness in various ways. Everything that brings us some level of happiness and comfort within this dream arises out of a *need*. A need to fill the void of Love. All of a sudden, I want to wake up. I want to fill that void with Truth. I want to remember who I am. I want to remember who my brother is. I want to see the Sonship in all of us.

ATTEMPTING TO MOVE FORWARD

Why have I had difficulty completing lesson 264? Though I love the thought of the lesson, I find myself straying from it during the day. I recognize that it must be my ego fighting this will to connect with the Truth. It is larger than I knew. I don't want to fight with it. Or do I? Is it because I still don't want to give up this dream? That can be the only answer. The dream seems to be saying, "Hey, over here, give me your attention." I guess I really do find the dream more important than doing this particular lesson. I mean, I have gone a few days before on the same lesson but never a whole week! The funny thing is I feel this is meant to be, and that I am supposed to get a very important message from this. The only thing that springs to mind is that for some reason this dream is very important to me, and maybe I am supposed to understand why I am that attached to it. Maybe I need to realize that this dream is still very real to me, and so being able to see the Love of God in replacement of the dream is a very difficult thing to do. For 5 minutes I can do it. But it really isn't all that easy.

It does seem that there are more important things going on in the dream. I'm not going to lie. One minute, I think I've got it, and that I am heading toward waking up, and then in the next minute I am swept full on back into the dream again. This dream just seems to take preference. It seems much more real than seeing even a glimpse of the Love of God. I need to only glimpse the Truth today. Spend some time on it. Otherwise, I will be stuck on lesson 264 for the rest of my life! Holy Spirit, please guide me here. I feel lost today. I realize I have an issue with completing this lesson. I want to get better at over-riding the ego. I want to get better at making less of this dream!

If I want to move forward with the Course and find my way out of this dream, then I need to get serious about this. Choosing between Love and fear is not something to take lightly. I must get good at choosing Love. I guess I have to ask myself is Love my choice today?

This feeling emerges from within that tells me, "Robyn, you can't have both. And you haven't made that decision yet. You are still choosing the dream throughout your day. Ask yourself at the start of each new day, 'Do I choose this dream? Or do I choose God?' You haven't opened the door enough to truly let the Light in. Don't be afraid. Nothing will hurt you. Your ego wants to protect you, but from what? From Truth! Truth will not hurt you. Truth will bring you home and you will never regret it. If your lesson takes you another week, a month, a year, that's ok. Time is an illusion anyway. But it has to be *your* choice to choose God over the dream. And you do have to make the choice before peace will be yours—before you can hold Truth in your heart again."

I pause to look at my lesson. **Lesson 264. I am surrounded by the Love of God.** [WB, pg 427] I am determined to make God more important than the dream. But, do I want this bad enough? I have no problem tapping into the Love of God. I feel Love everywhere and within everything. And for a minute or so everything else starts to fade. Love becomes stronger, more "knowing" than the fading symbols of fear that surround me. But after about a minute I feel the urge to surface and breathe again. It is not unlike holding my breath underwater. I can do it for so long, but it seems I can't breathe as well in this world of Truth. It feels that I have to go back to another world, the familiar world, so I can breathe easily again. Okay, I will not let the dream win! I want to know Love again. I want to know God again. I want it to become so familiar to me, so breathing feels odd in this dream!

Well, one good thing is that it does seem to get easier each time I tap into Love. I am starting to feel somewhat acquainted when I first enter Love's dimension. But to hold the focus for even a minute longer each time seems difficult. Like I still need to return to what I know and take that breath. But, the good news is that those additional seconds of connecting feel really good. It feels as though something or someone is teaching me to breathe, and those extra few breaths feel very refreshing. I do want to connect with this other "knowing" all of the time. I want to learn this.

I can see now why it has been so difficult to complete this lesson. The dream would keep winning, as I could breathe easier in the dream—this familiar world that I have come accustomed to. And it seems there is no way to change this feeling, this natural response, unless I change my habitual awareness. I need to learn how to breathe in this other world, and trust that I will continue to take that next breath.

As I pause to repeat my lesson again, I feel the trust building. That's what it is! Trusting that I am going to a better place! And trusting that this new place is safe. So then, what is it that makes this old place (the dream) feel safe? I guess a feeling of belonging. A feeling that it is home. After all, it is all we really know. We think the dream is all we have. But, at the end of the day, it is *all we know.* So then why wouldn't we think it's our truth? What makes it even more difficult is that we think we see, hear, taste, touch, and smell everything in the dream which makes it *appear* very real. And then, on the other hand, we can't see Love. We can't see God through these human eyes. We also can't touch God. We can't touch Love. We can't touch the other side! Just now, I begin to feel soothed as that song by Olivia Newton John comes on the radio in the background, "We have to believe we are magic...nothing can stand in our way... Destiny will survive." I smile to myself.

REMEMBERING IT'S JUST A DREAM

So this morning as I open the Workbook to look at my lesson, I feel the guidance that it is now time to move on to lesson 265. I suppose I feel fairly good about completing lesson 264. However, I am getting the feeling that it is not for me to judge and that Holy Spirit knows when it is time for me to move forward.

To connect with and come to know God's Love is truly the essence of this work. Each time I make God's Love very real then I decide that the ego is not. I can honestly say, however, that 99.9% of my day right now I am choosing the dream, especially where my relationship with Ian is concerned. I know I make our relationship very, very real. And for the most part I am not even conscious that I am doing it. Maybe I need to work at becoming more conscious that we truly are just playing around within some dream. Hmm, that kind of lightens the load a bit when I consider that it is *just* some dream. If I can continue to remember this then I can minimize any seriousness and just have some fun while I wake up!

FORGIVING THE DREAM

I have been considering the dream, and have decided that I want to learn to forgive the dream. After all, isn't that what forgiveness is? Seeing what was false and then releasing it, therefore forgiving the meaning we once gave it?

I don't want to, nor am I ready to, downplay what Ian and I have. I have a lot of respect for our love and sharing. I just want to become conscious that we are playing a game within a dream. Because then I can still enjoy it, respect it, and engage in it, while understanding the truth about it. This new thought system should actually create less drama, less worry, and less frustration. So, then when all that seriousness is minimized there will be more room for love, and more room for play.

Once before, I was scared of seeing the truth because I felt I had to release what Ian and I have. However, now I feel one hundred percent better because I know that's not the case. We don't have to release what we have. We just have to view it through a different lens.

I fully understand that there is some shift in awareness that must occur, and it won't happen overnight. There is much to relearn here as I work at no longer making real what seemed very real for 43 years. It will be a lot of work, but it seems to me that this is the only way to finally meet with my Truth. I have a feeling, a sudden urge, to go and put on Ken Wapnick's CD, called "The Happy Dreamer."

REACHING FOR THE HAPPY DREAM

Okay, after playing Ken's CD, I got a message that said, "Don't get the wrong idea about making *this* "a happy dream." It is more about seeing it for what it really is, and then lightening up. Not taking it all so serious. Instead, couldn't we just have some fun with it while we are here? After all, it is going to take a while to undo what has been done. To undo the ego that is. But wait, that's like a double edge sword...isn't it? The effort that will be required to make this happen will be based on a lot of awareness, and my ability to stay focused on the big picture...the Truth. I get the feeling that there will be double edged swords, traps, hamster wheels and dark holes along the way, all in aid of keeping me asleep that much longer. If I fall in a dark hole and happen to forget it's a dream, and my focus gets set on the dark hole instead of on the Truth, then there will be other dark holes up ahead. Projection determines that. It seems the ego knew all of this, and baited these traps eons ago so time would expand into what would seem like an eternity. Well at least I am aware of the plot now, and also understand that I must be patient while I train myself to become fully aware in each step. It will just take a while to get used to the fact that this is a dream and to take it more lightheartedly.

I guess I have been fearful up to this point in really seeing this for what it is...just a dream. I felt I was minimizing what Ian and I have and also minimizing the relationship I have with my Mum, family, and friends. But nothing is going to be minimized. I can see that now. Everything will be maximized in TRUTH. My relationships can only get better as I begin to see them with love and not fear. What can be so bad about that? At the end of the day, I guess the ego in me was always afraid of losing something.

I know it will take a while for me to convince myself that the dream-state isn't real and to take it all more lightheartedly.

But the goal is finally set. I also have to understand that Love can be misconstrued with the love of the ego. Or, I should say, the ego's replacement for Love. That is the neediness of love, control for love, etc. As long as I keep reminding myself it is all a dream, and then move forward with an open heart—a vulnerable heart—I really can't lose. I can only win what I have always wanted. And that is ongoing happiness, peace, and truth.

WEATHERING THE DREAM

The clouds have moved in today. And the last couple of days here in Lanikai have been quite windy. Apparently there is a hurricane somewhere out in the Pacific. Yesterday, I had trouble keeping my umbrella in the sand at the beach. I was feeling a little needy I must say for a strong man. Lucky Ian comes back into town this Friday for the weekend! I am really excited to see him again. I miss him a lot. I know that is my needy ego again. But that's okay. It is what it is. At least I know that. And I can allow the feelings to be what they are today. The shift will happen in its own way. But no matter what, I will always enjoy Ian's company as long as we are together. My feelings tell me I can be sure of that!

Between now and Ian's visit I want to work on making the conscious choice to see the Truth in him. I want to make the conscious choice to see him as me, and to see him as the loving Son of God. Guidance is telling me I must take a step at a time. The first step is to consciously see him as the holy Son of God. Joining with him as One feels like the next step.

Today in Lanikai I see white water piercing through the break in the trees from my lanai. The ocean here is usually quite smooth. However, the last couple of days it has become very choppy. It must be that hurricane in the Pacific. I pause to take a sip of my hot chocolate. I consider Hawaii and how much I love it here. Part of me wants to stay in Hawaii a bit longer. I am enjoying being here a lot. But Ian is not the type of person that will be in a relationship that is distant. He wants to be near, which makes a lot of sense. I can certainly relate to that. I miss him a lot when we are not together. We both enjoy each other very much, to the point where it does feel like we probably *need* each other very much. It's funny, because the "ego-love" relationship is all I ever wanted. And now it is in the palm of my hand. It's fun, it's romantic, and I adore Ian. However, I do understand that it is a relationship built on ego requirements. Not that that is a bad thing today. It just is what it is.

At times, I do feel like I am moving into a whole new time-zone with this Course in Miracles stuff. I don't even know how much I care right now about having the whole Cinderella story. Or maybe I do care. I feel that ACIM baffles Ian and even frightens him at times. I can't blame him. If the shoe were on the other foot, I might be running for the hills right about now! Sometimes, I can feel him hanging on while part of me slips into this other time-zone. I often wonder about this aspect of our relationship and how things will unfold.

I'm really tired right now, and I know that being tired brings disconnected feelings. So now is not a good time to search within for answers. I don't think Holy Spirit could get through even if He tried right now. I think I will go for a walk down to the beach and check out those white caps.

BATTLING THE EGO WITHIN

It is a warm morning in Lanikai. It is amazing just how warm it is here at 7 in the morning. It feels like the middle of the day! I love that about Hawaii. As I take a seat on my lanai, I begin to ponder the ego traps within this dream. Earlier I found myself getting frustrated as I began to feel like a prisoner within this dream. Fearful thoughts which cross my mind are so nicely painted and covered up at times that I don't realize it's the ego trying to keep me here in this dream. So, this morning I was mulling over this annoying realization and began to get very flustered with the ego. As I got more and more upset, I decided to let it know how I felt about it. So, in my mind, I said in a frustrated tone, "I can see that you send fearful thoughts through my head to try and keep me here! You want to stop me from going home. Well, guess what, you are not going to stop me!"

Just then, a strong wind came up. It seemed like it was the ego talking back to me. I stopped and said in my mind, "I don't care, you don't scare me. I am going to use the body you made to take me home! I will go inside the building you built to keep me warm. And if you knock the building down, I'll come back and do all this again. You won't win. Because I choose God! I choose Holy Spirit's Voice over yours! I'm done listening to your useless fears. They get me nowhere. You even tried to use my friend's drama the other day to keep me stuck in the dream. I can see that now! If I listen to your fears and abide by them, I will keep creating through them. I want to see the Truth! I want to *be* the Truth! You put shit in my head that makes me doubt Ian's and my relationship at times. You want to scare me and you want to scare him! I want to see my Truth. I want to see Ian's Truth. You can't stop me from remembering the Truth. I've started to recall it. And I choose God over you!"

I started to feel chills run through my body. Good chills. They felt really nice. My body shuddered. I have always recognized those types of chills as being affirmation from Spirit. Just then I called out to Holy Spirit (in my mind of course), "I want to be aware of the ego's efforts to keep me in this dream! Please help me to recognize the dark holes, the hamster wheel, and all the traps! *And please help me to remember at all times that this is a dream!*"

Chapter 13

Love or fear

A PEACEFUL SHIFT

Today is a new day, and I feel different today. Like something has changed. I feel less in control, but somehow in more control, which is strange. I feel like something has lifted from me—a burden of "not knowing" maybe. And I feel stronger, like an "inner knowing" has taken its place. It feels good but I know I will be tested again. I want to live in truth. But I have to be aware of what is false and what is true. I have to be *very* aware, so I can live in the "knowing" of the difference.

I love sitting on my lanai, reading, writing, and doing my lessons. The large plumeria tree overhead shades me from the heat of the tropical Hawaiian sun. And right now, due to the winds we have been having, there are plumeria flowers on the ground all around me. It looks so pretty.

I stop in my thoughts for a brief second to remind myself that it's a dream. A pretty picture that surrounds me, but alas, it's still a dream. I hear a lot of birds singing. I think they are calling out to each other to warn of the rain coming. You can smell the rain in the air right now. I think it is about to bucket down. I really like how the air is still very warm even when it rains here in Hawaii. The piece of ocean that I see through the trees is looking rough right now. That hurricane mustn't be too far away. Ian checked it on-line and said it is closer to the big island of Hawaii—so still quite a distance from Oahu. While I take in all of this beauty around me, I pause once again and become easily aware that it is all part of the dream.

I find myself day dreaming within the dream when my eyes become fixed on the ocean's white caps through the trees. Soon my focus drifts and settles on the cars going around the loop on the slope below me. I love to just *be* in these day dreamy moments. It feels good and I feel connected. As I surface from my dreamy state, and come back to reality—or, I should say, as I come back to the dream—I look around at my friends here on my lanai. There is the owl, a flamingo, a frog, and a few lizards. They are small garden statues, so all remain still amongst the foliage, except for the lively lizards. The flamingo is a couple of feet high, and sits in between me and a tiki torch. The flamingo has a name, "Mango." Prior to Ian's last trip, I was describing the unit and surroundings to him, and I called the flamingo a mango instead of a flamingo by accident. One of those blonde moments. Now, when Ian sees him in the background on "Skype" he laughs and says, "Hi Mango."

I have grown quite fond of Mango. He is a picture amongst the foliage. I have been trying to work out a way to ship "Mango" back to the mainland. Ian told me it isn't the right thing to do, as he doesn't belong to us. I told Ian, "Well if it's just a dream, does he belong to anybody?" I of course agreed and found out where they bought Mango and went to buy my own, but unfortunately, the manufacturer doesn't make him anymore.

It was near the end of Ian's last trip when he picked Mango up for a photo one evening, and dropped him. Mango laid on the floor in two pieces. I told Ian, "Now he's in two pieces, he will be easier to ship!" Ian smiled, and performed a guilty, magical surgery, and right now as I hold pen to paper, I look at Mango sitting next to me in his rightful place on my lanai.

I do like all of my "still" friends. I like the owl and the frog too. My still friends don't say too much, which means I don't have to deal with any ego while I read and write here. When I need an ear they tend to just stand and agree. Hey, wouldn't it be nice if we had a remote in our pocket and walked through life just pressing a button to mute the ego whenever we felt like it? Hmm, I suppose we kind of do but we just don't know it because we have handed so much power over to the ego. Wow, always learning. Lucky I enjoy this whole journey of learning. Right Mango?

THE SELFISH CAT

The past few days I have been spending some time getting a grip on this whole dream idea. As I sit on the lanai mulling over the dream in my head and all I have been learning a nearby branch touches my shoulder. I move suddenly. Was that to bring me back? To make me think this dream is real? But it isn't. Now I know it's only a dream. It doesn't matter what touches me or what I touch.

The cat next door (a gorgeous little white cat) came close before for a pat. I enjoy that little cat. He often runs by with his little bell jingling and looks at me as though to say, "I don't need you right now. I don't need a pat right now. I am going to lay in this corner and just rest." I love the selfish "knowing" of this cat. He knows what he needs and doesn't need in every moment, and he makes no excuses. Sometimes, I'll call him and he just looks at me and looks away. Sometimes, he will come to the door and demand my attention by meowing out loud. However, he only does what is best for him. No apologies. He can't hang around all the time, he has places to go and people to visit in his own selfish time. He's not all about pleasing my ego. And I like that about him.

The weather has settled today. I guess the hurricane must have moved on. The sun has been out most of the day and it has been nice and warm. So, as I went for a walk along Kailua Beach earlier, out came the sun block again, and lots of it. I love it here, even when it is rainy and windy, like the past few days. It is still warm in Hawaii when it rains, plus the rain seems to come more in spurts rather than for long periods of time.

I have been collecting plumeria's while doing my lesson and they are spread out across the table. Flowers always make me smile, and I love to smell these plumeria's. When I was walking before, I saw a red plumeria tree. I haven't seen one of them before, it was really pretty. When I live here one day I think I will have one of those red plumeria trees in my yard.

THE "PLEASING" EGO

When I consider the ego, I find myself wondering why the ego appears to be winning in holding this dream together. I suppose we give the ego so much recognition. We idolize individuals. We think authority figures have the answers. It is quite interesting to see that all of a sudden we are being controlled by a bunch of illusionary characters. We see the ego as brilliant; yet the brain is a part of this body—an illusionary part of this body. Hmm, so what does the ego know really? One day, when the book closes, and the universe disappears, how real will it all be then?

We seem to wear masks to make us appear like positive, happy people. And when we're not happy, we just find something to be happy about. Who are we proving our happiness to anyway? And why? Why do we care so much? Isn't it because we are trying to please the ego in ourselves or in others? Yesterday, twice, when I was in conversation with another, I felt the ego in me, like I haven't noticed it before. It was very subtle, yet it wanted to appear all of a sudden very nice. It wanted to be obliging, talk so nicely, answer so nicely, be so wise, and be so cool. I actually felt the disconnection as I was *trying* to be what I thought I *should* be. It was very interesting. I haven't noticed this type of disconnection in conversations before. For the first time, I was extremely aware of my "pleasing ego." I guess I never noticed it before because I just wasn't *aware* of the "people pleasing" part of me. But, recently, I have become more aware of the ego's fearful habits—*my* fearful habits.

The ego hides so much. We walk around disconnected so much of the time, and we have no idea why. We don't even know we're doing it. We are so lost, to the point that we are numb. It doesn't feel bad, it doesn't feel different, because it is what it is—a numbness that has taken over and made us completely forget who we truly are.

As I ponder these thoughts, I am reminded of a paragraph in my lesson today. **You will identify with what you think will make you safe. Whatever it may be, you will believe that it is one with you. Your safety lies in truth, and not in lies. Love is your safety. Fear does not exist. Identify with love, and you are safe. Identify with love, and you are home. Identify with love, and find yourself.** [WB, pg 425, 5.1]

Well, for now, I suppose I just have to continue convincing myself that this is all a dream. Also convince myself that safety lies in truth and not in lies. I know I seem to be doing a pretty good job convincing myself that all of this is a dream, but I also know when Ian arrives tomorrow and I am in his arms again, that the dream will feel just as real as it can.

ROMANCE WITHIN THE DREAM

Ian arrived back in Oahu last night for the weekend. It is nice to be with him again. We always have so much fun together. We both love the beach, the sun, swimming, snorkeling, kayaking, going for drives, talking, and walking together. We also love to learn together and question the Course together. Well, Ian questions it, and I sell it.

This morning Ian and I have been indulging in some warm, friendly, Hawaiian sunshine on my lanai. And now we are getting ready, with a bit of slip, slop, slap (an Oz term for sun safety—slip on a t-shirt, slop on some sunscreen, and slap on a hat—since we still believe that everything, including the sun, can harm us in this dream) then we are off to relax on Lanikai Beach for the arvo.

ENJOYING THE SUNSHINE

It is busy at the beach. It is Saturday, plus school holidays, so there are lots of people hanging out enjoying this gorgeous Hawaiian sunshine. I look up from my writing as the sun pierces the waters of Lanikai, producing the most brilliant light blue water that I have ever seen. It is truly amazing, and testimony as to why it has been selected many times over as one of the most beautiful beaches in the world! I look to my left and see Ian in his own world immersed in Jed McKenna's book.

As I gaze at the brilliant blue water, I ponder this journey I am on. I do want to get good at doing forgiveness lessons. I know that my relationship with Ian is a perfect opportunity. It is an opportunity to rise above things that happen and forgive. However, I catch myself pointing the finger. I don't forgive. Instead I make it real. I want to forgive all the time but it just doesn't seem as easy as 1.2.3. I wonder when I will be able to see Ian as myself and then forgive?

A feeling comes over me that tells me I am still giving power to the ego—I am still making this dream important. I then feel a gentle reminder to call on Holy Spirit each time I am wishing to forgive and He will stand with me and assist me in learning how to forgive.

As Ian and I collect the umbrella, cooler, and towels, I consider the possibility of waking up from this dream. I feel almost stunted right now. Like growth is impossible. But it feels impossible *only* because I continue to make the dream real. I know I can stop making it real and join with Ian. I know I can! This feeling surfaces that says, "Yes, Robyn, you can...and you will."

TIME FLIES WHEN YOU'RE HAVING FUN!

So, it is Monday already and Ian leaves tonight. I won't be far behind him. I head back to California in a few days myself. These past two months have gone by very fast. My time here has made me realize that I could indeed live here on Oahu. A couple of years ago I spent 3 weeks here writing and got a small dose of island fever. I wasn't sure if that might happen again on a lengthy trip of 2 months. But, thankfully, not a spot of island fever in sight!

Yesterday, Ian and I drove up to the North Shore and went snorkeling at Sharks Cove. We didn't see any honu's, but saw some colorful fish, and had a lot of fun. Later in the arvo, we drove around to Waimea Bay. It was surprisingly smooth and great for swimming. The last couple of times I've visited Waimea Bay it was very rough. Ian said that it is rough in the winter months, and smooth in the summer months. I like it a lot better in the summer I decided. Last night, we went to our favorite restaurant for dinner, Buzz's. We always have a great time there. And today we are just going to take it easy on the local beach here at Lanikai.

I figured that since Ian has become an integral part of my journey, and a part of this book, it might be fun to introduce him to you. So when he arrived the other day I asked him if he would like to share something from his last visit with us here in this book. I was surprised when he didn't need a second invitation. Straight away he said he knew what he wanted to share, and off he went to put pen to paper. So, we'll have to wait and see what he is eager to share with us in the next chapter!

SWEPT UP IN THE DREAM...AGAIN

I haven't done my lesson in a few days. Gosh, at the rate I'm going, I will be lucky to have these lessons completed in this lifetime! So, here's my guilty-ego story. In the past few days I have allowed myself to be swept up in the dream...again. Ian was here and I was enjoying Hawaii so much with him and knew our time here together was limited so I just laid my lessons aside. Yes, just closed my Workbook. I thought it would be okay to do that for a few days. However, I can see now that I have fallen off track, and understand what some teachers mean when they say that some begin to wake up and then get sucked back into the dream. It kind of feels like I saw a spot of light, and then the darkness got a chance and quickly took over again. That is exactly how I feel—like the growth stopped. And no room for any light to enter because I got so caught up in the dream. Okay, I am going to run off and do my lesson right now, and make that my priority today.

STAYING ON TRACK

So after spending some time this morning on my lesson, I am feeling somewhat back on track. When I am back in California in a few days, I hope my relationship won't get in the way of me completing my lessons. It wouldn't be because of Ian, he allows me all the time I need to complete my lessons. However, it could happen if I choose play time with him over my lessons. Or, in other words, choose the dream over "going home!"

As I sit and ponder "how to stay on track," I get the feeling that I need to keep my focus from straying too far from the truth. I get the inspiration to pick a quote each day relating to the truth, and repeat that quote over and over so it stays with me. For example, "This is but a dream," (as I look around me) I say, "This is but a dream. This is but a dream." I look at the dream and see it as that and repeat it for a minute or so.

Each day I will be inspired with a quote. As I sit here and digest this I can already think of many quotes that I would love to have imprinted into my mind. For example, "Ian is the son of God. I am the son of God. God's Love is everywhere. Holy Spirit is always with me." I am excited about this because I seem to fall back into the dream state quite easily. And I continue to make the dream real—especially where Ian and I are concerned. I enjoy the depth of love we share. But I can feel neediness for each other setting in. It is early, five months into the relationship; however, I do want to begin to see Ian as his Truth. And I do want to develop a holy relationship with him.

GOODBYE TO LANIKAI

The time has come. It is time to say goodbye to Lanikai and goodbye to Hawaii. Tomorrow I head back to the mainland. It is bittersweet; I get to see Ian again every day back in California, and that thought makes me smile. However, I must also say goodbye to Lanikai...and Hawaii. I don't know when I will be back this way again, so I am a wee bit sad.

I have learned a lot while here in Hawaii. Something about this place seems to help open a vortex to Truth, and allow Higher Knowledge to flow through me. I feel prepared for the next leg of my journey now, and feel that something here has prepared me for that. Today, I am learning to put a lot more trust in something larger. That larger knowing I identify as Holy Spirit. I feel that here in Hawaii I have come to know and connect to Holy Spirit on a far deeper level than I ever could have imagined. I know that this friend will indeed come with me on the plane tomorrow, and will be with me for always.

Chapter 14

A Note from Ian

THE ARRIVAL

After residing in California for fourteen years, I have had the opportunity to visit "The Islands" many times. I still feel it a privilege each time I visit. As a boy, who grew up in a small provincial town in Northern England, Hawaii appeared to be a mythical land of far away. Our vacation spots back then seldom involved travel of more than two hours by car. Hawaii seemed about as close to me as the moon, so my visits here are never taken for granted.

The warm, tropical air immediately makes its presence felt as I exit the plane. The smell of exotic flowers fills the air as new arrivals around me are greeted with traditional lei's. You have a sense you are somewhere special!

I joined Robyn halfway through her 2 month writing project, just because 2 months was too long for us not to have time together. Even though we have been seeing and talking to each other over the internet every day, there is no substitute for being in the presence of your loved one.

Robyn was at the airport to meet me, lei in hand of course, which was my first, and a very nice touch! We took a leisurely drive around the coast to Lanikai, stopping at various points along the way to take in the awesome views. When we arrived at Lanikai, I understood why Robyn had talked so often about the place. It was quite picturesque and the perfect place to experience island life.

The following morning we awaken to July 4th. So we did what many good Americans do on this Holiday (well, a transplanted Brit and Aussie) and we spent the day at the beach. It was obviously busy with people barbecuing, swimming, and generally enjoying the day. The sun was so much warmer than back home and the turquoise colored ocean was almost impossible to stay out of. That evening we watched the Kailua fireworks that were staged on a barge in the bay. The weather was not playing its part as there were intermittent showers; however, it didn't dampen the show. Watching fireworks on a bluff overlooking this magnificent beach in Hawaii was something very special and was certainly a romantic ending to my first day in "The Islands!"

The following few days came together perfectly. We went snorkeling with honu's. We kayaked out to the small islands off Lanikai, called "The Mokulua's." We also hiked to the peak of nearby mountains which offered the most magical and panoramic view over all of Lanikai and Kailua. Hawaii has so much to offer and we were making the most of it.

AN INVITATION TO CONTRIBUTE

I enjoyed spending time in Hawaii with Robyn so much that I decided to visit again toward the end of her two month stay. It was on this second trip, as we sat on the lanai outside of the apartment reading and chatting, when Robyn surprised me by asking if I would be interested in sharing an experience from my first trip to Hawaii in her book. As soon as the words came out of her mouth, the story I wanted to share was already forming in my head. I was feeling excited about putting pen to paper, although I have to admit I also felt a little apprehensive about the prospect of exploring my writing capabilities, as I had never before considered writing for publishing purposes.

Robyn and I have had many conversations about life and how ACIM has affected her thoughts on the subject. She actually introduced me to the concepts of ACIM and, though at this stage I do not consider myself a student, I am fascinated by its message and how it seems to answer many questions that I have had in my life to date.

At the start of our relationship, Robyn appeared to be like any other woman, though I was soon to find out how different she was. She was, of course, extremely attractive to me and had a wonderful, carefree attitude that was immensely appealing, yet in the beginning she did not disclose her interest in the Course. As our relationship and comfort level grew, she became more open about the work she was doing and the teachings she followed. Like myself, I suspect that to most people this would have been a bit of an eye opener, especially when she started to explain to me that everyone else's life and mine were but a dream! Of course I challenged this theory with my usual bravado; however, as she explained more I became increasingly interested. As I look back over the years, my interest, unbeknown to me at the time, appeared to lie mainly in dealing with the release of the ego. This was something I acknowledged when I revisited my poetry, and found that the sentiments behind the words revealed my awareness of, and frustration toward, the ego.

One afternoon, we walked along what they call the "loop," a single road that winds around the tiny town of Lanikai where we were staying. This tiny enclave has some of the most exclusive homes on the island; some of which belong to the rich and famous. The beachfront homes were certainly impressive and stretched along white sandy shores for about a mile. As we strolled along, admiring the views, I looked up into the hills rising behind the town and noticed people on top of, what must have been, at least a 1000ft hill overlooking the ocean and town below. We both agreed that we needed to take a trek up that hill to check out the view for ourselves.

THE STORY

Now to the story I was asked to write. This perfect sunny morning, we were pottering around and hanging out on the lanai amongst the palm trees and green tropical shrub with Mango the Flamingo, Brat the cat, and Larry the lizard (friends around here are pretty scarce) while indulged in our usual discussions around "going home." This was still a new concept for me. Even though I felt intuitively knowledgeable about the topic, it was still a learning process. I suddenly remembered the hill and suggested we go climb it. Robyn, in her usual adventurous fashion, agreed immediately.

I grabbed the local map and tried to figure out the nearest access point for our climb, and then off we went. Two blocks from where we were staying, we came across a small road where I thought the trail might start. I looked around and couldn't see anything. Robyn pointed out a tiny path between some bushes and a chain link fence and was confident that was the way. Initially, I was skeptical, however, went along with her idea, and was soon to find out that sure enough this was the way. The path was very narrow, and with loose dusty soil as the base, it was not the most secure footing.

It soon became steep, so much so that there was rope strung between narrow saplings that was supposed to be an aid. It didn't seem strong enough to hold anyone's weight I thought as we scrambled up the now rising incline. It then struck me that we were massively under prepared for this adventure, with no water, no cell phone, and what was worse we were both "underdressed" for the occasion. Robyn had flip-flops, a bikini with a small sarong tied around the waist. I just had board shorts and flip flops. Not the best attire to climb what turned out to be a pretty significant hill.

So there we were on this small steep path and neither of us with the slightest hesitation to continue. As soon as we started to climb the steep incline Robyn began to feel her feet slip and felt uncomfortable. I took her hand and began helping her up the slope. She soon told me she felt more comfortable to take the rope, and she loosened her hand from mine and reached for the rope. This didn't sit well with me. I have always been the kind of person that likes to "protect." Robyn has mostly been someone that trusts her gut instincts and in this instance she felt the rope was safer than my hand. I felt she had no confidence in my ability to stop her from falling. This of course was purely an egoic thought. Why should I *really* care if she chose the rope over my hand? Well, firstly, I was programmed to protect the fairer sex from an early age, like open doors, let the lady go first, be polite, and all that "stuff" that was drummed into many of us from an early age by parents, teachers, and anyone else who thought they could make an impression. When this is rebuffed in a situation where you feel you can provide some sort of assistance it hurts, or rather it hurts the ego. Robyn, on the other hand, felt she was safer using the rope. She was not ignoring what felt right to her. Not for a second. She tried to appease my obviously hurt ego by telling me she needed to do what "felt" right to her. However, I had a problem as to why she didn't trust my help. Despite my understanding of her decision and how she felt, my ego was still bruised.

This situation was my first insight into how things might unfold with *A Course in Miracles*. Would Robyn become so advanced and enlightened that the rope (signifying the Course to me) be more significant in her life than me? Would she almost become detached from feeling any sort of reliance on me in this "new order?"

I let the rope incident go after a couple of mumblings of discontentment under my breath, which of course I made sure Robyn heard and to which she greeted with a knowing smile that somehow comforted me.

We pushed on up the really steep slope until we reached flat ground and our first peak over the edge toward the ocean and Lanikai below. We both stood there a little breathless yet in awe of the view that lay below. We hadn't realized how high we had climbed but we could see the village below in all its glory. Not to mention the colorful ocean and the magnificent twin islands called "The Mokulua's" that were famous in the region and were synonymous with the view from Lanikai. We were seeing them from a whole new vantage point now, removed from the flat perspective at beach level and viewing them from what seemed like the heavens. I have always been drawn to views and especially from heights. I feel it gives a new perspective. It offers removal from the norm into a more inspiring and, as Robyn would say, connected state.

We didn't say much, other than ooh's and aah's at how beautiful the view was. During our climb some people passed us as they trekked down the hill. As they approached, Robyn asked how the climb "up" was. They said the climb got easier. Good I thought! No need for her to hold on to that bloody rope anymore! Another ego thought that was trying to mend itself after the apparent bruising it had received further down the hill.

We continued our ascent. The path did become much easier and we soon reached the summit. The views were nothing short of spectacular. The ocean was bright blue with the shallow reef clearly visible below the water. We could see right around the coastline, and the volcanic mountains rose behind us like monolithic statues from an age gone by. We climbed onto what must have been a World War II lookout bunker—a small concrete building that looked out over the Pacific. I thought of the people that would have had to climb up the hill to reach this spot and spend hours looking out to sea. Hmm, yes, there were worse jobs to be had I thought!

RELATING TO THE COURSE

As we stood and looked out onto the massive expanse of the Pacific, my thoughts wondered back to one of the conversations we were having about ACIM. Robyn had been talking earlier in the week about how the ability to see Love in *everything* was key in understanding ACIM and in moving forward to going Home. Up here on this bluff it was relatively easy to *feel* the Love. It was peaceful, beautiful, and an idyllic situation, especially with Robyn by my side.

But what about the real world? I by no means consider myself an intellect, not by a long way, but I do think I have an enquiring mind and for years have asked questions like most of us. For instance, "Why are we here?" and "What is innate versus what is taught?" and "What makes me who I am?" So when I hear some of the teachings of ACIM my mind goes into question mode.

Seeing the Love in everything is a "nice" way of dealing with the world. I question the ease of this, but of course nobody said that ACIM was easy. I work in a pretty fast paced environment and trying to incorporate the teachings of ACIM could be difficult at best. I don't think I have *really* tried yet, but I can see that it would be. So my mind turns to visualizing certain situations and how I would "see the Love." I guess "seeing the Love" in essence is to rise above the ego, however, as I have found, this is not easy. Robyn and I have had run-ins with ego. We have discussed situations where the ego has risen within us and we need to be aware of wrong-minded thought. As a novice to all of this, I somehow see this process very clearly but staying focused and aware of these situations is challenging. Even when ego is manifesting itself in us and making us feel bad, it still feels comfortable because the alternative of ignoring it is too alien to us.

Throughout a lifetime, the familiarity with the ego offers the illusion that it is our friend. I have thought how, on occasion, I get embroiled in egoic thoughts and feelings. If I get stuck in this quicksand of egoic thought it would be helpful if someone could throw a line and not let me fall deeper into wrong-minded thought. I know this may sound dramatic. Even though I have struggled with the concepts of this, the more I am understanding ACIM and also becoming aware of these egoic thoughts, the more I understand that this ego stuff is something that requires attention. It requires constant attention to how you are relating to those around you and how your "feelings" are being affected and delivered.

I have no right to be lecturing about this. I still have my training wheels on when it comes to ACIM. However, I say to those of you that might be experiencing ego difficulties in a loving relationship—and your partner is an ACIM student and you may not be—it's tough to understand, but if you are willing to learn, you will find that just knowing that it is ego at work trying to trip you up is very useful. Also, knowing not to take anything personal helps. One thing I am sure of is that our relationship has a firm footing, an ability to communicate and understand each other, which is a requirement I feel necessary in a romantic relationship when it comes to eradicating ego.

When people are caught up in wrong-minded thought it's NOT as it seems, it's false. Yes, someone might appear to be upset or hurt but those feelings are coming out to be healed and dealt with. It's not real. It's ego keeping us in the dream. Of course, when we are in ego mindset, we don't want to hear this but it is what we need to be mindful of in the moment.

I have contemplated why Buddhist monks disappear into a life of solitude. When you think about it, it's pretty obvious why. They too are looking to dissipate ego. Ego is far simpler to contain and manage when you: 1. are not in a loving relationship 2. have little or no interaction with fellow man, and 3. reduce external influences in your life. I always knew that Buddhist monks were smart and now I know why. They make it easy for themselves!

So, back to seeing the Love in everything. This, I believe is the state of being at "one" with everything, and therefore is the place where the ego finds it most difficult to inflict its power. It's a place of peace and tranquility where only good resides. That's why when sat on top of this hill with Robyn, and while looking at the magnificent view, it was easy to see that.

This Course stuff sure is an eye opener. It does make perfect sense to me—especially on a day to day basis when dealing with the ego and the emotional ups and downs it brings. I am a long way from understanding the whole concept of ACIM, though I do feel that without any pushing or cajoling from Robyn, I am beginning to embrace these teachings and understanding what is behind the principles. It's all about going home and this message is relayed in many religions. However, ACIM seems to have struck a chord in me and is something I relate to.

We took many pictures from the top of our World War II bunker. After a while we decided to make our descent. Robyn was a little concerned that going down would be more treacherous than coming up. We both paused again when we reached the first level spot and looked down at the steep part; we then turned and nodded to each other as if we were charging into some kind of medieval battle.

As we approached the section with the ropes, Robyn was still holding my hand but as the slope became steeper she eventually succumbed to her intuition and made a leap for safety and grabbed the rope. I was fine this time, knowing her intuition would reach out for it. Even though I think she held on to me for as long as she thought safe to make me feel better. I couldn't resist letting my ego out by making some sort of comment about why the rope should be safer than me. Robyn has a knack of dealing with my ego. She knows the right things to say and how to act when my ego is in full flight. Just her smile alone can send the ego scuttling back to its lair, knowing that he has no "game" when faced with the disarming smile of a beautiful woman. Anyway, we both made it down the section without mishap, and we were pretty pleased with our accomplishments considering how ill-prepared we were.

So, this was the story I chose to share with you, mainly because it came to my mind immediately. However, I also think it demonstrates, in a very mild way, an example of the types of issues we all face when it comes to dealing with ego. This was obviously a minor occurrence, though I believe in time Robyn and I will have the skills to become more *aware* of what is required in being fully equipped when dealing with the ego. And, who knows, we might even learn to have fun with it along the way!

Chapter 15

Putting the Learning into Practice

REFLECTIONS

I hope you enjoyed Ian's story. I had fun reading it. We had a great time together climbing to that old war bunker. It was definitely a highlight of my trip. Lanikai beach is already quite breathtaking from the ground, so I really didn't imagine it could get any better. I could have sat there on the top of that bunker all day with Ian taking in those incredible views.

Looking back, my two month trip to Hawaii was what I was hoping for and more. I loved it all, and it was especially fun when Ian visited. So, here I am back in California. I arrived last weekend. Until I get myself located here, Ian has kindly invited me to stay with him, which I gladly accepted, and must say am enjoying every moment with him. Since my return to California, I have been spending some time reflecting on the two month trip and am realizing just how much my attitude toward life has altered.

I don't feel so attached to the dream these days. That doesn't mean that I don't make it real. For the most part, I still make it very real. I don't always remember that it is a dream. But when I do remember, I find myself letting go of it. I think I am quite sold on the fact that it is a dream, and now it feels like there is no turning back. I mean, I don't think that tomorrow someone can come along and encourage me to disbelieve all that I have now learned. I still need to put all my learning into practice but moving forward I feel I am ready to begin disembarking from the dream.

I have also been considering the importance of Holy Spirit's guidance. If I allow myself to be guided by Holy Spirit always, then why would I ever need to worry about anything? Holy Spirit isn't going to guide me down the wrong path. I'm learning more each day that everything happens for a reason and I just have to relax and know what I am guided toward, when it feels right of course, is the way I am meant to go. So what do I have to be afraid of? Really, at the end of the day, what do I have to be afraid of? The worst thing that can happen is that I croak it. And if I do, I am not really dying anyway. So, why do I get fearful at times? Fear makes me want to control situations. It makes me want to take the steering wheel back.

I love Jed's story, at the beginning of his third book, "Spiritual Warfare." He is running from the police, and when confronted by one who pointed a gun at him, he found that death was the least fearful thought on his mind. He knew he wasn't a body, and he knew he wasn't really going to die.

Come to think of it, it seems that death would actually be the easy way out. Then we wouldn't have to do the work of dissipating the ego. But we do need to do the work at some point, or in some lifetime, when our choice is to wake up. So I might as well get good at handing over that steering wheel and following Holy Spirit's guidance today. What makes me think that I know best anyway to take that steering wheel back? What do I know? I truly *can't* see the outcome. But Holy Spirit can. Holy Spirit knows how to get me home, and what I need to go through for that to happen.

THE WILL TO DO FORGIVENESS LESSONS

I feel that I should be doing forgiveness lessons daily right now. But I also feel like something is holding me back. To actually stop myself in the moment and do a forgiveness lesson just feels so alien. I know that fear is stopping me. And I know that I am making everything real. But why do I do that? I seem to have difficulty doing them at any time.

I am angry at the ego right now. Part of me wants to dissipate it quickly. Dismantle it like there is no tomorrow, and then deal with what's left. But is that the answer? As I feel myself beginning to reconnect, this feeling comes over me that says, "Robyn, hand back the steering wheel. You have the steering wheel right now."

LATER THAT DAY

I felt disconnected most of this morning, so I decided to take a walk along the beach to work at getting reconnected. As I walked, I considered this journey I am on. This is some journey. I realize that there is Truth, and then there is this other thing—this ego—that doesn't want me to know Truth. I feel trapped some days. I feel like there is no way out. Then, thankfully, I get reconnected, and always remember that there is a way out...forgiveness lessons!

I find it difficult to do a forgiveness lesson in the moment when I should be doing one. Earlier, on my walk, I was thinking about forgiveness lessons and my relationship with Ian. I found myself considering the fact that we are One. So, if he is the same as me, then why would I ever want to hurt him? I feel how precious he is. I feel his beauty. I know how amazing he is. And deep down I know he is the Son of God. I only want to see him as that! I don't want to see him as anything else. However, the ego within wants me to see him as something else, and wants me to see him as very separate from myself. How can I rise above this Holy Spirit and move into my Right Mind where the Truth exists and stay there?

A FEW DAYS LATER - RISING ABOVE

The past few days Holy Spirit has been guiding me to recall and put into practice all I learned in Hawaii. I have also been discussing things with Ian. And these past few days we have come to a better understanding of our relationship with each other, and how the forces of the ego, plus the desire to dismantle the ego, affects both of us.

Lately, Ian and I seem to get tested every other day. It is like the ego knows it's going down, and it is trying to wave everything it possibly can in front of our faces to keep us from going home. The good thing is we know this. We stop a moment and say, "Hey, got sucked in again." After ego has had us for dinner, and sometimes desert and coffee too, we take a step back and have a look at our relationship and help each other to "understand" how we got sucked into becoming part of the ego's key ingredients yet again.

It helps to talk about it. And after all, we both want to "dismantle" the ego. We both want the same thing. So, we are not out to hurt each other. We each know that. And to know that Holy Spirit keeps reminding each of us how beautiful we are at "Truth level" helps tremendously. Thank God for Holy Spirit! That connection to our Truth! Each time we pull back one more layer of ego, we turn around and find a stronger connection with each other. Like there was something we didn't know before, but now we join and now we get it.

There are so many facets of the ego. And all these facets appear in all different colors and in all different ways. They appear, do their work, then disappear, and just when you think they are gone, they reappear. It is then that I realize I have fallen off, over and over, because I haven't forgiven this wrong-minded thought, but instead made it real...again.

I see the facets of the ego in their purest colors. I get what the ego is doing. I am catching myself in ego-mode. I catch myself taking the steering wheel back. I catch myself wanting to control things. I catch the ego doing what it does best—trying to keep me stuck in this dream!

DISMANTLING EGO

When I was 28 I backpacked Europe, as many Aussies do. If you have backpacked anywhere in the world, you know what I mean...we are everywhere. I think many Aussie's are born with a backpack on!

When I backpacked Europe, I felt as free as I had ever felt in my life. Not one person knew where I was. I didn't have to answer to anyone. I felt so much harmony for so many months. Today, I look back and see that I was fleeing from the egoic wrong mind. Don't we all want to do that? I love Ian's honesty. He says he doesn't like people. He would prefer they leave him alone for the most part. I thought once for an instant, "Hmm, well, that includes me." But then realized he is only referring to the ego. I am surprised he didn't become a Buddhist monk. Well, if Ian ever goes missing, I guess I know where to find him—scrubbing floors and praying somewhere in Tibet!

I see the ego, I am understanding the ego, and I want to dismantle the ego. Yet, I get caught in ego. It is as though it has a hook, line, and sinker all ready for me, and I am the fish and it just continues to bait me. The problem I have is recognizing "in the moment" when that bait is dangling in front of my eyes. Sometimes I don't recognize it until I have already taken the bait and it has firmly attached itself to my wrong mind. I would love to recognize it immediately. And say, "Thank you, but no thank you." But for some reason I continue to take that bait!

I heard you Holy Spirit last week when you told me how amazing Ian is. But the ego's voice was louder in judging Ian. And then it was loud in judging me. And yours was this subtle, little, gentle voice, that just pops in for a cup of tea once in a while. It seems that the ego is just so powerful. I don't want to resign to the ego's power any more Holy Spirit! When will I choose Love, and Love is ALL I will see?

I must keep reminding myself that when Ian "appears" to hurt me, it is really *me* hurting myself...because of my wrong-minded thoughts. And on the flipside, when I "appear" to hurt Ian and feel guilty, it is just a facet of the ego trying to make me believe that there are two of us in the room. All wrong-minded thoughts are really coming from *one* wrong mind. Okay, so I need to get this stuck in my head: *There is only ONE of us, and I am doing everything to myself!*

QUESTIONING THE FAITH

Obviously faith has a lot to do with this path I am on. When I trust Holy Spirit with the wheel, I can then be guided to do forgiveness lessons and be guided home. How much faith do I really have in Holy Spirit? When I trust Holy Spirit with the wheel, it seems that all unfolds for the best. Abraham (Law of Attraction teacher) used to say "You will be guided in bliss."

157

But, sometimes I feel myself wanting to take that damn wheel back because I think I know best. Deep down I *know* that Holy Spirit knows best. I know it. But sometimes, for some reason, I lose faith—I cease trusting in Holy Spirit. How do I gain complete trust in you Holy Spirit? I want to trust you one hundred percent with the wheel.

This feeling emerges that says, "Robyn, you *choose* to trust me with the wheel. Only *you* make that choice. Have you made that choice?"

I do want to make that concrete choice. I want to trust you one hundred percent Holy Spirit *all the time.* But then, what about Ian? I would love to walk this path with Ian, and maybe you will end that relationship? I guess I have to trust that you know best. I know you brought him to me when I handed over the wheel initially. So, if you knew best back then, what makes me think I know best now? It feels right to be with him today. It feels that we are on a similar path and heading in a similar direction. I have to know it is the ego part of me that questions what you would do. And I have to learn to trust you with the wheel and know that no matter what happens it will all unfold the way it is meant to unfold.

CHOOSING HOLY SPIRIT

This morning, I have been thinking about the steering wheel and how I can become more *aware* when I have it in my hands. Most times when I take it back, I have driven around the block a few times before I realize I have it firmly in my hands. I do want to become more aware when I have my hands on the wheel. I pause to do my lesson. **Lesson 270. I will not use the body's eyes today.** [WB, pg 430] I read on to paragraph 1. *Father, Christ's vision is Your gift to me, and it has power to translate all that the body's eyes behold into the sight of a forgiven world.* It makes sense that if I remain in control, I can't forgive. Because who is in control? The ego is. I either give Holy Spirit the wheel or I keep hold of the wheel. When I keep hold of the wheel it means I am giving the wheel to ego! It is my choice. If I can let the wheel go I will see with Christ's vision instead. Then I can be led to a forgiven world. We really do think we are the body. It makes sense why we want to be in control! Okay, so another good quote for the day is "I am not this body." I have heard some Course teachers say the body actually flourishes when we stop controlling everything and do our forgiveness lessons. So we don't need to be concerned about our bodies. They will take care of themselves. But when we know we are truly *not* our body then we can release the power the body thinks it has. The power of control!

Chapter 16

A Closer Look

STOPPING US IN OUR TRACKS

Ian and I had a show down last night. And guess who the lead character was? Hmm, yes, the ego. Front and center stage. And its performance was a whopping 10 out of 10! It stopped us in our tracks and we sat down and asked each other what was going on. We both know we love each other so much and we don't want to feel this kind of discomfort in our relationship. We questioned the situation, however, due to the fact that we wore each other out with our arguing we were too exhausted to come to any solution. And do you think a forgiveness lesson was anywhere in sight when the ego was having a brandy back-stage? No way!

When I was upset at Ian, Holy Spirit tried to guide me toward a note I put on the fridge last week. I felt the gentle nudge and the quick sign of my eyes glancing at the note. However, disconnection continued to take over as my frustration grew.

In my state of "wrong mind," I continued to argue with Ian. The note said: Ian is Love, Robyn is Love.

This morning Ian sent an email and said, "I know what I am going to do. I am going to see you as Love. I am going to stop focusing on egoic stuff and only focus on the Love." I had just sent him a quote I received from Ken Wapnick that read, "Our outer surroundings are a sign of an inner condition." It made us both think. As I received the email from Ian, I had just been thinking in my mind the same thought, I need to see Ian as Love and stop making the ego so real.

If we are producing a stage play based on our "inner condition," then we can *only* be doing it to ourselves! There is one Son, and therefore, there can only be one egoic thought, separated into many. The separation becoming greater with every fearful thought added. So, we really are doing everything to ourselves! My mind, in its "wrong state," is producing a stage production. And the players really don't matter. Because it *has* to manifest, it *has* to occur. And I am only doing it to *myself.* No-one else is doing anything to me! In every moment of every day I am creating my own stage production. I am the "lead" character and all the other players are an extension of *myself,* revealing what is in *my* wrong mind.

As I do my lesson, I turn to the Theme of Special Relevance number **6. What is the Christ?** This particular line about Christ gets my attention: **He is the Self we share, uniting us with one another, and with God as well.** [WB, pg 431, 1.2] I think of Jesus, and the fact that we are all "One" including Him as the Sonship. My thoughts cross to Ian, and I feel him as the Sonship also. I see the Love in Ian, and then turn to feel it in myself. We are all ONE! And then everyone else I know are all One with me! No-one is left out. The Sonship is One, divided at the wrong mind, into "many." The "many" portray the ego as the wrong mind, that's all. Separation is only the decision

NOT to know ourselves—a quote I wrote down at Ken's seminar last year. I wrote it down. But until now, the true meaning of the separation hadn't sunk in. I never really knew exactly what the separation meant. I mean, I did at an intellectual level; I got it, it made sense, but now I really get it at a *knowing* level! The separation is only the decision NOT to know MYSELF!

I read on to paragraph 2.1. This paragraph makes me think. **Christ is the link that keeps you one with God, and guarantees the separation is no more than an illusion of despair, for hope forever will abide in Him. Your mind is part of His and His of yours. He is the part in which God's Answer lies; where all decisions are already made, and dreams are over. He remains untouched by anything the body's eyes perceive. For though in Him His Father placed the means for your salvation, yet does He remain the Self Who, like His Father, knows no sin.** [WB, pg 431, 2.1] Wow, this makes me want to really know myself now, as the Sonship. I have to cease believing that I am separate. When I remember that we are all joined as One, then, why would I ever choose to see sin in myself? And why would I ever choose to see sin in any other? Because *everyone* is ME!

When I see someone in egoic expression, I can stand back and say, "He does not know who he is." And then I can choose instead to see the Truth in him. I can choose the "Sonship" over ego. In every moment that I do that, I will return home one instant more. Every time I can forgive "egoic wrong mind," I can release that wrong thought in myself. For I must remember, when I see another in egoic expression, it is only a reflection of *my* wrong mind. The projection from my wrong mind is the reason I am there in that moment witnessing the event or conversation.

It is exciting to know that Holy Spirit is assisting us here. We only have to "know," and "be aware," and then "choose again." Holy Spirit will do the rest! **The Holy Spirit reaches from the Christ in you to all your dreams, and bids them come to Him, to be translated into truth. He will exchange them for the final dream which God appointed as the end of the dream. For when forgiveness rests upon the world and peace has come to every Son of God, what could there be to keep things separate, for what remains to see except Christ's face?** [WB, pg 431, 4.1]

I pause to repeat the first sentence and allow it to sink in. **The Holy Spirit reaches from the Christ in you to all your dreams, and bids them come to Him, to be translated into truth.** Lately, I have felt an acceleration of learning. Could it be that Holy Spirit is drawing the illusions through me in an accelerated fashion, as I have focused more on "going home" in the past weeks than ever before? As I consider this, I realize that I can't lose sight of the fact that a great opportunity exists right now—the opportunity to forgive these illusions that are showing up for healing. As I look at these illusions and stop making them real, then Holy Spirit can finally take them from me, correct them, and from what I understand, once corrected, they will never mean the same to me again.

FORGIVING SPECIAL RELATIONSHIPS

I have been back in California a few weeks now. The other day, Ian asked me to stay on permanently instead of getting my own place. I smile as I write this. Our relationship does make me very happy. It *feels* right to be with him. And I want to follow Holy Spirit's guidance, so it appears I will be staying on with Ian. Being together all the time means we will have that much more fun together! Hmm, then I guess on the flip-side, it also means we will have that many more forgiveness lessons together!

I've noticed recently that almost *everything* I come across in my day to day life requires a forgiveness lesson. That is because everything I see around me is part of this illusionary experience, of which I have made real at some point. I suppose I must forgive special relationships and no longer make them real also.

My thoughts go to Ian. It's like I realized in Hawaii, the ego-love is all I ever wanted for as long as I can remember; now I have to learn what love *truly* is. To dissipate the ego-love feels like I must go through a type of mourning. It makes me sad to release the type of "needy love" that I thought I always wanted. A part of me wants to continue to feel those feelings of specialness, but another part of me wants to keep preparing to "go home" also.

I have to make my choice. I can make my relationship the way I want it by telling Ian my needs and then also work at trying to fulfill his. Or, I no longer stay attached to the outcome of this relationship. Meaning, I would have to "give up" all my needs, all my desires, and everything I *think* will make me happy. I would have to hand over the steering wheel entirely, and make the neediness redundant. It's almost like I would no longer care. And that makes me sad.

I stop to consider the outcome of giving up special relationships. In the Course it says when we accept opportunities to forgive wrong-minded thoughts, which arise in any relationship, we then accept healing. Healing turns a special relationship into a holy relationship. A holy relationship does sound pretty neat.

Just then a feeling comes over me that says, "Robyn, you are yet to glimpse how precious a holy relationship can be. The love you share is maximized by truth. It will gleam, it will blossom, and it will grow. Special relationships only wither and die, don't you see that? Special relationships wither in fear. Holy relationships grow in love. Have faith and you will see."

UNSTICKING THE NEEDINESS

I have spent a lot of time today thinking about special relationships and the neediness that keeps me stuck on the hamster wheel. It is not always so easy to see when I am stuck. Sometimes it feels okay in the moment and I have no idea that I am stuck. I find this happens mostly with my romantic relationship. My other relationships with family and friends don't seem to affect me in quite the same way. I suppose this does make sense as our deepest needs seem to surface in romantic relationships.

Today I have come to realize that there is a clear sign offered via our actions and reactions that give indication of the ego neediness. As soon as I say "you," as in "you did this," then I am staying stuck. When I catch myself requesting a different action that causes a need within to feel better, then that is coming from ego, and will only keep me stuck in the dream. Well, that is quite the task: to have absolutely *zero* expectations when living under the same roof as a loved one. That means *anything* they say or do that may appear to affect me is a-okay. Hmm, well nobody said this was going to be easy.

I turn to my lesson. My lesson today invites me to remember the sinlessness in my brother as in myself. **Lesson 274. Today belongs to love. Let me not fear.** [WB, pg 433] I read on to paragraph 1. *Father, today I would let all things be as You created them, and give Your Son the honor due his sinlessness; the love of brother to his brother and his Friend. Through this I am redeemed. Through this as well the truth will enter where illusions were, light will replace all darkness, and Your Son will know he is as You created him.*

MAKE SPECIAL OR MAKE HOLY?

Am I ready to make my relationships holy? I realize I do make *all* of my relationships around me special today. It does seem that all my loved ones are outside of me. However, I have to begin to see them differently if I am choosing to make them holy relationships. I have to see everyone I know as a reflection of me. And I have to see them as a reflection of what is happening in *my* mind. All of these reflections are being shown to me so I have opportunity to forgive. They offer me an opportunity to see the illusion and stop making every aspect of it real.

If I make any type of relationship more important than going home, then I will stay stuck. I have to forgive *every single aspect* of the dream. When I make the choice to let each error (wrong-minded thought) fall away, by no longer making each one real, I am giving up the dream bit by bit and allowing Holy Spirit to correct my mind bit by bit. In every moment of my focus I am either choosing to stay stuck longer or I am choosing to "wake up" sooner.

Chapter 17

Forgiving my Brother and Myself

FLORIDA AND FORGIVENESS

It is late August, and Florida is hot, hot, hot this time of the year. Ian and I are both accustomed to very warm climates and even these muggy types of weather conditions suit both of us just fine. We are staying in Fort Lauderdale, which is about an hour's car ride north of Miami. The coastline is colorful here and there is an abundance of waterways leading into residential pockets. It is a very pretty place.

Ian is at a business meeting right now, so I am enjoying some relaxing time by the pool. I look at the time and realize I must go pack for our trip this afternoon. We are driving to a friend's place on the West Coast of Florida. They live in an area called Redington Beach, which sits on the outskirts of Tampa. Fortunately, Ian and I have many things in common, and one of them is that we both like road trips.

When I was a child, my parents would round us kids up at wee hours of the morning, bundle us into the car, and embark on long road trips to fun destinations. Every Xmas, as far back as I can remember, we would go to a place called Narooma. Narooma is this adorable little town in Southern NSW, which, I would say, holds some of my fondest memories as a child.

We would drive south from Sydney and meet my Nana, Poppa, Aunty, and two cousins who would drive up from the state of Victoria. Narooma was like the half way mark.

For many years we shared a large old home perched up on a hill, overlooking an inlet of water, bearing a small uninhabited island. A thin, wobbly, old walking bridge granted access to this small island, where my cousins and I would spend most of our time either fishing or playing amongst the mangroves, crabs, shells, and sand.

Hopping in the car and driving with my family to Narooma was always exciting. Thoughts would fill my head of days that lay ahead filled with fishing, swimming, hiking, and playing. The road trip was always eventful, comprising of travel games. The games included ones like, "Who could spot the most windmills, or "Who could get through the alphabet the quickest," by locating letters on billboards, signs, and car number plates. This afternoon, Ian and I will be crossing Alligator Alley. Maybe we will play, "Who can spot the most Alligators!"

THE ROAD TRIP

Ian has arrived back from his meeting. It doesn't take long before we throw the suitcases in the car and we are on our way. We are both excited that he has finished work and a road trip adventure lies ahead.

The roads are quite busy as we leave Fort Lauderdale. It is 3 o'clock on a Friday afternoon and we have caught the rush hour traffic. The map that we have, for some reason, doesn't show the adjoining freeway for Alligator Alley. After driving around in circles for a while and feeling trapped in traffic, we both begin to get frustrated. We look at each other and say, "ok, FL." We use the initials FL when we say a "forgiveness lesson" is due. It makes us smile when we realize together that this moment is something to forgive and take lightheartedly.

After a FL, and locating the correct freeway, we peacefully begin to leave city life behind and enter wilderness territory. A few moments pass and I can tell that something is on Ian's mind. He explains that he is thinking about forgiveness lessons. The other day, we had an interesting conversation about forgiveness lessons and it appears that conversation has remained on his mind. They are obviously a huge part of the Course, and it seems that Ian is developing quite an interest in them. As we approach Alligator Alley, I get a feeling to ask him if he's willing to share these thoughts with you, the reader, about forgiveness lessons. Ian's graciously agrees.

FORGIVENESS INSIGHT IN ALLIGATOR ALLEY

Okay, Robyn, but I think you had better dictate, or I can hand over the steering wheel! Okay, forgiveness lessons. I have heard Robyn talk about these for months and I'm not really clear yet what purpose they serve or exactly how you do them. I have a slight understanding, and attempt to do them as best I can. I know that forgiveness is obviously a good thing; however, what is the process you must go through to truly forgive? The concept of forgiving is a strange one for me.

Earlier, we did a forgiveness lesson in the traffic. Well I think I did mine? It felt kind of good. It got me thinking today about the concept of forgiveness and the important role it appears to be playing now in Robyn's life.

After our forgiveness conversation the other day, I feel I am beginning to somewhat understand the process of forgiveness. I definitely get that it isn't as simple as saying, "Okay, I forgive you." But I want to understand more. I have some questions. Perhaps as we drive across this alligator infested wasteland we can discuss this and I can learn some more about the process of forgiveness and what this ultimately achieves.

I have been a "fly on the wall" watching Robyn take this journey. Sure we have talked about many aspects of the Course, and sometimes I feel like I am doing the Course myself, but as you know I have barely picked up the book. However, you can't help but get involved when you are close to someone who is doing the work.

I get the feeling that doing the forgiveness lessons is a big key to implementing the teachings of ACIM. I suppose if you forgive everything then you carry nothing around—no baggage, no judgment, no expectations—and that would be nice. So, when the desire is to wake up, learning to do the forgiveness lesson's appears to be more than important—it's a must.

Recently, watching Robyn's journey, my interest in forgiveness lessons has grown. As we drive, I begin to quiz her about them. I ask Robyn if she could explain in more detail how I would complete a forgiveness lesson when something is bothering me. Robyn explains there are steps involved in completing a forgiveness lesson. Well, I think I am sold to the point where my interest has peaked enough to want to learn these steps. So I ask Robyn to clarify them. On our drive, I made a mental note of the following steps:

Step 1

Recognize a wrong-minded thought – fear-based (any thought that causes me to feel uncomfortable). Invite Holy Spirit to stand with me and assist me in seeing the Truth.

Step 2

Understand and acknowledge that this wrong-minded thought is illusionary and was brought about by my own dream-state projection. Pass the wrong-minded thought to Holy Spirit for correction.

Step 3

With Holy Spirit's guidance, I then choose "Love" instead. I feel the Love (for example, join with my brother as One). I recognize my Truth, and choose Right Mind.

As we get deeper into the conversation I begin to see how all fear-based thought can be negative, and the way to eradicate this is to acknowledge and forgive the wrong-minded thought. I can't help thinking though that this could be some kind of magic roundabout. I can see myself constantly caught up in wrong-minded thinking and going round and round on the forgiveness merry-go-round. So, how do you know the wrong-minded thought has been eradicated? Will it come back again? Will I find myself forgiving the same wrong-minded thought? Robyn tells me she has forgiven the same wrong-minded thought multiple times. She said that Inner Guidance tells her this is ok and to just continue doing what she is doing. I understand that this is an ongoing process but boy does it seem like a lot of hard work. I certainly feel I will be spending a lot of time doing these forgiveness lessons.

As we continue our discussions I notice a big, and I mean BIG, black cloud up ahead. It's rainy season in Florida and I think we are about to get a taste of it. We are here at the tail end of a hurricane. The force of nature is a magical thing and I was secretly hoping to experience at least a little of it while we were here, and the big black ominous cloud up ahead just might fulfill my desire. We continue another mile or so and it is becoming noticeably darker. I tell Robyn that this looks a little serious. She's noticed. Just then big blobs of rain begin to hit the windshield...and then more. Before I know it I'm in the biggest downpour I have ever witnessed. At first it was really cool, but now I can't see where the hell I am going. Luckily the freeway is relatively empty. I slow right down and move over to the right-hand lane. Going at 25mph I can barely see the road. My windshield wipers are on turbo setting, hardly having any effect on the torrential rain. Even in this downpour, other drivers, who are obviously more used to these conditions than me are traveling at crazy speeds. I wonder what they can possible see in front of them as I can see diddly! I'm generally a fast driver myself but even for me these conditions are extremely dangerous. Hmm, is this one of those wrong-minded thoughts? Should I be doing a forgiveness lesson?

We continue our slow progression and after the downpour subsides we get back to our forgiveness discussion. Robyn explains that if we follow the steps in forgiveness then it will help in the transition to us waking up. I am having a few problems with all of this. Not only do I see this as one big forgiveness merry-go-round that may never stop; I also have difficulty seeing how this will lead us to an awakened state. In the past, anyone I ever perceived as being "awakened" or "enlightened," I immediately gave reverence to, due to the fact that they must have witnessed something life-changing and way beyond my comprehension. But is it really like that? Maybe we have held this awakened and enlightened state in too high a regard. Maybe this is something "normal" people can achieve. Maybe I don't have to shave my head and drape myself in an orange robe and eat rice for the rest of my life! Maybe I just have to forgive!

BACK IN CALIFORNIA

Yesterday Ian and I returned home to Hermosa Beach. Florida was a lot of fun. We visited our friends in Redington Beach who took us boating on the intercoastal around St. Petersburg. The intercoastal is a maze of charming residential waterways. Another pretty spot in the dream!

Today's lesson is **lesson 277. Let me not bind Your Son with the laws I made.** [WB, pg 435] Relationships, in my mind, have always appeared to be a "give and take" experience. It seems that in each relationship the ultimate desire is to make one another happy. I have always found this to be an accepted role in any relationship. So, I struggle with today's lesson. I read on to the first paragraph. ***Your Son is free, my Father. Let me not imagine I have bound him with your laws I made to rule the body.*** Last weekend, in Redington Beach, Ian decided he wanted to jump off our friend's balcony into the shallow end of a swimming pool. My eyes not only saw the minimal depth of water he was jumping into but also saw the length of concrete between him and the pool's edge. My feelings cried out "no." I saw him in my mind not making it. As I saw him getting ready to jump, I quickly grabbed him by the shirt and pulled him back from the balcony then told him not to be crazy. Later, Ian admitted to me that he had considered jumping, but for the most part, was merely testing my love for him. Hmm...yes, the ego can be cute at times! Another FL. Today, I look back at this situation and say, "What part of me wanted to stop him from jumping?" It had to come from fear. Isn't that a form of control? I wonder what I would do again in a similar situation. It would be difficult to stand by and say nothing if I thought a loved one was about to do or say something that could cause him or her harm.

This feeling surfaces from within that tells me, "Robyn, when you stand in fear, you separate. When you see the Son of God in Ian then you join in love and you will be guided to offer a loving response in that type of situation. What you choose in Ian, you are choosing in yourself. If you choose ego in him, you choose ego in yourself. If you choose Love in him, you choose Love in yourself. When you choose Love, you will be guided to say what feels right in a situation like that, rather than standing in fear."

I can see how the fear in me is a powerful device with a will to control outcomes. For some reason, I feel like I just met that ego part of me for the first time. That part of me that Holy Spirit is speaking to in order to get me out of this dream. Or, maybe I just realized what my ego presence truly is. That part of me that wants to pick up the steering wheel and be in control. That part of me that feels I know best for "me." And feels it knows best for "everyone." That part of me that feels *so* real...but really isn't.

SEPARATION

I am beginning to understand that separation is what causes all of my pain. Ian and I saw a topic differently last night, and we had our own opinions and views. We debated what we each believed to be correct. The debate soon became heated and created a feeling of "separation." Now, on this new morning, I look back on the situation and all I see is "separation." And for the first time ever, I look back on something that appeared negative and realize there is nothing to be said about the heated debated topic. There is no talking required to make it all better. There is no communication required at all. Because today I look back on last night and I see ONE of us creating a separation. That's all I see. My heart tells me today there is nothing to fix. It tells me there was only one of us in the room last night. ME. There appeared to be two of us debating. But there was only one of us in the room. So, there was one projection coming from what appears as multiple facets of the wrong mind. Those multiple facets are an illusion appearing real to the ONE Sonship. I look back at the turn of events, and I see and feel the insanity of the wrong mind. I see how I am fast asleep in this crazy illusion. I see that it is all *my* projection. It is all about me, and nobody else. Ian is me. We are ONE as the Son of God. It is almost startling to come to this realization that there is absolutely *nothing* to fix.

I love Ian dearly, and the Truth in me never wants to hurt him. We can't let the "separated egoic mind" win. I am determined to remember who I truly am. God created me in his image. God created me in the image of Love. I am the Son of God. I am all that is pure and holy. I can do no wrong. Ian can do no wrong. We are ONE.

This morning I was looking at the paper on the fridge, where it says, "Ian is Love"..."Robyn is Love." I grabbed the pen and wrote in little words all over it, "ONE...ONE...ONE" and then I wrote on the bottom of the page, "And we are ONE."

I guess releasing this dream was never meant to be easy. It is like the wrong-mind is made of concrete. I seem to wake up a little some days and then fall sound asleep again the next! But concrete wears and dissipates over time right. So I can break down this wrong-mind! I can give up my attachment to "fixing" things. Only the ego fixes. Only the ego analyzes. There is only one thing to do here. See my own projection and realize that *everything* is that...*my very own projection.*

WHO IS APOLOGIZING?

I hate it when Ian and I argue, as I know he does. We have so much love between us that it kills us both to emanate any ill feelings. So now I want to hold him and apologize for ever

175

hurting him. But I have to ask, "who is apologizing?" Surely the ego, right! Because that part of my wrong mind wants me to believe that "I did something wrong." And then the guilt sets in. And there I go again, in that egoic, cyclonic, insane behavior pattern. It goes around and around, from blame to guilt. If we're not feeling blame, then the ego goes, "Okay, well if he didn't do it, then you must have done it. See, someone must have done it!" The egoic mind always sees separation. And if separation were in fact true, then someone must have done it. Someone must have been guilty!

When I see that we are all "one" then I can see clearly how projection works. The wrong mind is being projected again and again in various facets of fear, all stemming from that original "wrong choice." So all we have to do is choose again and JOIN with our brothers. No-one is left out. No-one is ego. No-one is bad. The ego is an illusion. It is a wrong thought that continues to this day. That wrong thought has created every ill feeling that has ever existed. That one error can now be eliminated. All we have to do is "choose again." We need to know there is ONE of us, and laugh at the silly mad idea of original wrong-minded error, and then turn to LOVE. At the end of the day the answer is really very simple. The answer is "choose again"...*and this time choose Love.*

Chapter 18

Finding Faith

I CAN BE HURT BY NOTHING BUT MY THOUGHTS

Everything I see is a projection of my own thoughts being played out. It doesn't matter how they are being played out. The original error continues and continues until I change my mind...from wrong mind to Right Mind.

I pause to repeat today's lesson. **Lesson 281. I can be hurt by nothing but my thoughts.** [WB, pg 438] Okay, I get how my thoughts are bringing me what I focus on. However, to live and breathe this every minute of every day and say, "There is no-one outside of me, and I am doing everything to myself," is not so easy to do. It is becoming quite apparent to me that my ego has a strong grip on this dream and doesn't want to let it go!

This knowing soon surfaces from within that says, "Robyn, the dream is important to you. You still think it's very real. Focus on your Truth. You are the holy Son of God. Keep reminding yourself. And when you believe wholeheartedly that there is only 'one' of you it will mean the end of the ego. How can the ego survive if it can't point the finger at another and make them separate from you? How can the ego survive if victim and victimizer no longer exist?"

This helps a lot. It makes sense that I have to go beyond all knowledge to the heart of my Truth. Nothing matters more than the Truth. And when I believe that I am indeed the holy Son of God and I am joined with all my brothers' then why would I point the finger? I will realize I am only pointing it at myself. And it would seem ludicrous to do that! Yes, when I come to this realization it makes sense that everything will come unstuck. The egoic mind will come unstuck. It will have no mental glue to hold it together anymore. Everything must fall away! I pick up my lesson and repeat it. **I can be hurt by nothing but my thoughts.** *Everything* I see and hear around me is a projection of my thoughts. I read from the first paragraph. ***Father, Your Son is perfect.*** This sentence feels good. The Son really is perfect. And the Son can only appear to do wrong from my own false-minded projection. I have to keep reminding myself that everything I see or hear is *my* projection. There is only ONE of us and everything I think about I am projecting outward from *my* mind. I am only hurting myself. Nobody else is doing anything to me. I believe this now. I just have to start living it. I have to stop being the victim and stop being the victimizer. Every time I choose to be a victim, I blame my brother. And every time I choose to be a victimizer, I end up feeling guilty. When I get good at this and continue to remind myself *it is all me,* then no longer will I play victim and no longer will I play victimizer. Instead, I can stand back and as Ken Wapnick reminds us over and over, "I can laugh at this silly mad idea." This silly mad idea of that initial thought giving birth to wrong mind being replayed and replayed and replayed. It is a projection of *ongoing* fear from the wrong mind. That's all it is.

178

FINDING FAITH IN HOLY SPIRIT

I keep reminding myself that Holy Spirit will be "with me" every step of the way, for better or for worse. Today's lesson's Theme of Special Relevance is **7. What is the Holy Spirit?** [WB, pg 437] I read on to the first paragraph. **The Holy Spirit mediates between illusions and truth. Since He must bridge the gap between reality and dreams, perception leads to knowledge through the grace that God has given Him, to be His gift to everyone who turns to Him for truth. Across the bridge that He provides are dreams all carried to the truth, to be dispelled before the light of knowledge.** Holy Spirit is the bridge home. How important is it then to remember Holy Spirit's presence in our lives? I do want to go home; therefore, I must walk across Holy Spirit's bridge from wrong mind to Right Mind. When I remember that nobody is doing anything to me and I am doing everything to myself, then Holy Spirit can correct my wrong mind and bridge the gap so I can live in Right Mind again.

I read from paragraph 5. **The Holy Spirit is HIS gift, by which the quietness of Heaven is restored to God's beloved Son.** [WB, pg 437, 5.3] Holy Spirit is my angel, my guide home. I choose Holy Spirit's guidance every day. I choose the Light across the bridge. I accept God's gift.

RELEASING FEAR

I am told that all fearful thoughts are not real, but then I look around me at the projected images of my wrong mind and they still seem *so* real. I wish I could know Love like I know the dream. This dream does feel very comfortable. Everything in it feels comfortable. Everything I see, hear, touch, taste, and smell feels so normal and so comfortable to me. And now I have to give it all up for something I can't see! I wish Love was this comfortable to me. If I am the Son of God and my essence

179

is pure Love then why doesn't it hold some memory? At times it really does feel as though I'm jumping off a cliff as I do this work!

A feeling comes over me that gently tells me to look at my lesson for today. **Lesson 282. I will not be afraid of love today.** [WB, pg 438] Another feeling follows that says, "You are afraid of Love, Robyn. And the reason you are afraid of Love is because you do not remember yourself, so you do not KNOW Love. How can you be comfortable with something you do not know? You know fear. You are very comfortable with the ego. You are comfortable with controlling and judging. That is what the ego teaches you. As you relate more to Love, those fearful thoughts of 'ending the ego' will soon dissipate. Each time you feel that feeling of jumping off a cliff, do your forgiveness lesson on that ill feeling and pass it to me. I will translate it to truth. But you must do your forgiveness lesson first. You must see it as a false idea about yourself. You must see it as a diversion from the truth and as something that is holding you back from going home. Remember, face any fear that you feel, and then choose again."

TO SEPARATE OR TO JOIN

I have read that it is okay to do a forgiveness lesson later (after the event) as long as the forgiveness lesson takes place at some point. However, if I feel angry in the moment, aren't my angry thoughts projecting a similar scenario again—which will call for another forgiveness lesson? It seems I am in a never ending battle with the ego right now. I turn around, and here comes another wrong-minded projection! Bam! Part of me wants to end this ego struggle right here, right now, for good. The struggle of "you did this to me," (blame) to the struggle of "now I feel really bad for getting angry" (guilt). The never ending battle of "victim turns victimizer."

Ian asks me, "What do we do when we disconnect in our relationship?" I say we can face the pain and do a forgiveness lesson, or we can ignore the opportunity to forgive, then blame the other person, and in time possibly end up moving on to another relationship that makes us feel good for a while until the same ego crap resurfaces. We can either heal it now, or we can walk away. If we walk away, we face healing it another time...or another lifetime.

At times dissipating the ego can be hard work. Ian and I were fine for months, and then as soon as I got serious about wanting to go home wrong-minded stuff just came from out of nowhere! I guess I have been asking powerfully to correct the wrong mind. But, today, do I want to slow it down? I don't know. Holy Spirit, here is the steering wheel! Please steer me in the right direction. I don't know what is best for me. Is my wrong mind going crazy because I want to find my way home? I don't know what to do. I am trying to hold my head above water here. And Ian says, "What should we do?" I feel like sometimes I can barely help myself. Holy Spirit, I need some guidance. I feel like a sinking ship and I don't know where the shore is! I feel blinded at times.

Holy Spirit, I know you don't judge me. It makes me sad that all I ever thought I needed was a romantic relationship—a romance to fill the heart and make me smile. Well, there goes that fairytale! So now I'm told relationships are a bridge to help us home. That's if we are gutsy enough to battle the ego. Because the ego is waiting on the bridge! The ego waits right there. It knows we want to go home. And it has all the tools out of the box. It knows how to loosen this and cut through that. It knows all the tricks to make us fall right off that bridge!

The wrong mind seems so powerful right now. But I won't let it get the better of me. I will remain strong. And I will continue to do my forgiveness lessons.

A feeling immediately arises that say, "Okay, let's do one now, Robyn!"

Oh, okay. I take a deep breath, and pause for a moment to feel Holy Spirit standing with me. I then say to myself, "I feel fearful that I am being held back from doing this work. It is my own projection. So it is me holding myself back. These fearful thoughts aren't real. They are part of the wrong mind. I don't choose these wrong-minded thoughts. I choose Love instead."

Chapter 19

From wrong mind to Right Mind

SHIT HITTING THE FAN

So, just when I think I might be getting a hold on this work, shit hits the fan again this past weekend. And this time it really hit the fan. The ugly traits of the ego ended up all over the house. Ego had weaseled his way in through the front door, the backdoor, the windows, and even came down the chimney! Something happened that neither of us were expecting. As Ian and I argued we became physical and started shoving each other. Straight away we realized this had gone too far and a silence drifted over the house. And neither of us could see a glimpse of light for hours.

I "asked" through my sadness why this was coming about. Why were me and Ian, two people who love each other very much, doing this to ourselves—especially when each of us hadn't done this kind of thing in past relationships?

It was later that day when the Voice within told me, "When you fought as young children you saw each other's actions as very real. You learned as children to physically dominate each other. This was the ego's way of revealing its so-called power." When I heard this, I understood straight away what Hold Spirit was telling me. It made so much sense. Ian and I were projecting out our childhood squabbles!

Understanding this made it so much easier to recognize the ego at work here. And why I had to once again forgive the wrong mind and see that no-one was to blame. It was no-one's fault. We were acting out what we had learned as children. And I guess, through adulthood, we had each decided that this type of behavior was wrong and possibly the reason why it hadn't occurred in previous relationships. Of course we also didn't want this to happen in our relationship. However, in seeking forgiveness opportunities, I suppose all the deepest, darkest stuff is going to come up for healing, including any and every projection from years gone by, that we each had made real.

Okay, so here goes my forgiveness lesson. I have done a number of forgiveness lessons already today on this one, but I feel to do another one right now. I stop to quiet my mind, and call on Holy Spirit to stand with me. I then say, "This behavior is coming from my wrong mind. It is my own projection. There is only one of us in the room; therefore I am only hurting myself. I choose Love instead of this." I take a moment to join with Ian and feel our existence as One—as the holy Son of God. Hmm, that feels a bit better. Each time I have done a forgiveness lesson today, I have felt somewhat better.

THE EGO GETS IN ANY CRACK

Later, after the disconnection occurred between Ian and me, we looked back and saw how the ego worked itself through

184

every little crevice. We saw how we blamed each other in ways that we normally wouldn't when connected.

Right after the fighting, this fear came over me, telling me, "This is tough—all this stuff that is surfacing. You and Ian surely can't handle all of this! How can you stay together?" When I hear this, I do get scared that we won't be able to get through it. And then this other feeling urges me to keep going. It tells me, "That egoic part of you just doesn't want this dream to end; it wants the dream to live on."

I know in my heart, as I sit here today, that the wrong mind won't stand in my way. Ian said before that he doesn't feel the threat. He knows in his heart we can get through this. It feels good to have a partner that is encouraging and positive in times like this.

I pause to do a forgiveness lesson. I call on Holy Spirit and then say, "This fearful feeling I have that Ian and I can't handle this work is coming from my wrong mind. These fearful thoughts aren't real. Holy Spirit, I give you these wrong-minded thoughts and I choose Love instead of this." I pause and take a moment to see and feel the Love flow to me and through me.

UNDERSTANDING THE IMPORTANCE OF FORGIVENESS

I am starting to realize just how important forgiveness lessons really are. As I ask to dissipate the ego, stuff is surfacing that is difficult to believe exists in my mind. But nonetheless, it exists, and needs dissipating if I want to continue on this journey toward home.

So, I ask myself, "How important is it for us to maintain focus and not overlook *anything* that arises?" Who wants wrong-minded thoughts hanging around? When old, old stuff surfaces, it can be shocking, and when made real, is immediately demanding projection once again. And the blunt truth is that we had better be ready to forgive, because if we're not, then what? This old stuff will only continue to resurface seeking projection yet again and again! It reminds me of one of those games at an amusement park. The one where they give you a bat, and those little furry-headed guys pop up and you have to be quick and try to hit one on the head before he sinks back in the hole again. This whole forgiveness journey reminds me of that. An old projection resurfaces and if you are not ready to hit it over the head, it will go back into its hole and resurface when you least expect it. So, if we are not ready to forgive the little demon popping up, then it will just go back to where it came from (to our wrong mind) to re-project at yet another time. And the re-projection continues. Until one day we go, "Oh, yeah, that little furry-headed ego guy is phony. He is just make-believe." And then we turn around to look at the Truth instead and just laugh at the silly mad idea.

Ian and I were discussing last night how difficult it has been on both of us with this old childhood stuff resurfacing. We realize how much we need to nip it in the bud before it has a chance to resurface and escalate. We both have been doing forgiveness lessons. So let's see how this unfolds. My gut tells me we are in for some heavy stuff over the coming months. And then *hopefully* things will get easier.

FORGIVING THE BODY

Over the past few weeks I have found it easier to do forgiveness lessons, and I am becoming more and more fine-tuned in the way I am doing them. Recently, my lower back has been playing up. So I have been doing forgiveness lessons on it. Today's lesson helps me to see why my back shouldn't be a problem. **Lesson 294. My body is a wholly neutral thing.** [WB, pg 445] As I do my lesson, I realize that my body has no meaning. It is neutral. It only has meaning as I give it meaning. If I release all meaning then I release all judgment on my body. And then my body can be used as a tool to take me home. With neutral thoughts, how can my back suffer? It can't. With neutral thoughts, there is no "projection." All suffering is of the wrong mind. So if I continue to do my forgiveness lessons each time my mind goes to "pain in back," then those wrong-minded thoughts will heal, and soon enough my back should be neutrally well. No more projection, no more pain.

I do think it is necessary to state that I am not minimizing the importance of medical assistance in situations such as this. For me personally, I feel it is a good idea to seek medical assistance for all physical ailments and/or discomfort. I receive the medical help that is recommended. I also do my forgiveness lessons.

Today, I can actually feel quite a difference in my lower spine. It feels better than it has all week. I have caught myself in wrong mind a number of times throughout the day and stopped to do a forgiveness lesson. After doing a number of forgiveness lessons this week, I can tell that my lower back doesn't seem to hold the same level of importance as it once did.

It feels good to remove importance that we place on the body and replace it with a knowing that "all is well." I have learned through doing forgiveness on my back that that is exactly what I am doing. I am removing the importance I once gave it—the judgment that I once gave that portion of my body. I stop making it real and hand over the old judgment to Holy Spirit. And it does feel really good.

I mentioned this earlier, and I think it is important to mention it again: I am not talking about pushing the negative thoughts away and ignoring them. I did that in PF1, and it is not so different than just sweeping them under the mat...only to re-emerge later, when focus is offered again. Not long after I started doing the Course, I received guidance from Holy Spirit to stop pushing away negative thoughts, or in other words "controlling my thoughts" during the day. The guidance was telling me to face the negative thoughts instead of pushing them away and feel what each thought meant to me. I didn't understand why I was getting this message from Holy Spirit at the time. However, I later realized that this caused me to identify the pain that came with the thought, which then caused me to *choose* Love instead of the dream. Then I would pass the thoughts that didn't feel good to Holy Spirit for healing.

I am not saying that PF1 (deliberate/selective focus within the dream) is incorrect. It certainly isn't, and offers an ability to harmonize thoughts and feelings while still believing in the dream. I would prefer that rather than living in disharmony each day within the dream. However, when we are ready to exit the dream, PF2 (the Course) offers us the tools for correction and dissipation of wrong-minded thoughts rather than just harmonizing them.

DAILY FORGIVENESS

In PF1, I had learned to "ask" to be *aware* of my thoughts throughout the day, and it worked. I would catch myself going into negative thinking. Prior to that, when I wasn't so aware, I would stay in negative thinking and continue to project those thoughts into the future. So recently, within PF2, I have been asking Holy Spirit to help me be *aware* of wrong-minded thoughts throughout the day, so I could catch myself...and this time do a forgiveness lesson.

Yesterday, as I headed to an appointment on Wilshire Blvd., I exited the 405 freeway and had difficulty getting over to the left-hand lane. As I slowed to await the passing cars on my left, a car behind me (who also just exited the freeway but needed to remain in the exit lane to take the next right-turn) sounded their horn to make me move out of their way. As I turned, I saw an irate woman glaring over at me. I felt anger begin to rise within. I then instantly recognized my wrong-minded thinking and remembered my forgiveness lessons. I took a deep breath, called on Holy Spirit, and as I looked at this woman I then realized she is my projection and I am offering this anger to myself. There is no-one out there. It is all my projection. I took the responsibility. It felt good. And as I felt Love replace anger I said, "I choose Love instead of this."

THE HOLY CHRIST IS BORN IN ME TODAY

As I move through my lessons, I am noticing the shift in my perception. A feeling within tells me I am exactly where I am meant to be. And my lesson today seems to mark a poignant place in my journey. **Lesson 303. The Holy Christ is born in me today.** [WB, pg 451] As this "knowing" arises from within that I am the holy Son of God, I reach out to loved ones in my world and all of a sudden, today, for the first time, I feel their Truth. I see beyond their bodies as if they are not really there. And I see "me" in each and every one of them. All of a sudden I see me everywhere. Bodies, words, and actions all seem irrelevant. The feeling of the *Truth* is what seems real. The rest is just like a fading dream. Today, as I do my lesson, I feel the "Oneness" that we all share. And surprisingly, for the first time, the joining feels effortless.

This past Saturday, Ian and I were discussing how we feel about each other after going through these initial stages of forgiveness. We were cuddling on the sofa while watching TV and it felt really nice. It feels like a new love is starting to emerge that wasn't there before. Not that it wasn't great before, it was, however, now it seems like a new type of love is emerging. One I hadn't witnessed before. And it felt *really* nice.

In our connected state, we do have a lot of respect for each other, so when we get upset with each other and shout at each other, it is painful. However, this old stuff from wrong mind must surface and we are very aware of that. Actually, these days, after we have calmed down, I start to appreciate the fact that I was just given an opportunity to heal. I know I have so much to gain. As long as I reach out and "forgive." This is the most encouraging thought I have had for a long time in regards to the Course and the work involved. I am beginning to feel I *can* make this shift...and I *will* wake up to my Truth!

Chapter 20

Finding Forgiveness at Last

FORGIVING THE APPEASING SELF

Summer has ended. However, today was a hot, hot day; it was 85F at the beach and 100F when I jumped on the 405 freeway. It is hard to believe that we are nearing the end of September already. As I drove to the doctor's for a check-up on my lower back, I was considering how much better it is feeling lately. The Voice within tells me to keep doing my forgiveness lesson's and they will continue to make a difference.

Ian and I were talking earlier of how we appease ego around us. We are both people pleasers from long ago. And we both got really good at it along the way. I feel the freedom coming through as I continue to do my forgiveness lessons on "appeasing." At Gary Renard's seminar last weekend, he shared some ideas on forgiveness lessons. Since then, I have been using a couple of them in my own life. This following type of forgiveness lesson has helped me with my appeasing ego: Each time I feel conflicted with the *need* to "people please," I would offer the person's body to Holy Spirit. In my mind, I would see their body float away in a bubble/balloon. I would feel the Sonship within them remain beside me, while the ego that wants me to please them is whisked away. Each time that feels really good. And as I continue doing those types of forgiveness lessons, I am finding a better "connection" with the people I have wanted to appease.

THE EYES OF CHRIST LOOK ON A WORLD FORGIVEN

The eyes of Christ look on a world forgiven. In His sight are all its sins forgiven, for He sees no sin in anything He looks upon. [WB, pg 457, lesson 313, 1.4] As I read this in my lesson today, I stop and recall the past. I have at times asked Jesus to show me how to see a person or an experience through His eyes. And it would work. I would be offered a feeling or an inner knowing.

Today, as I do my lesson, I get a feeling to ask Jesus to show me what it looks like to see Ian as sinless and forgiven. In the next instant, this feeling comes over me providing me with a vision of a loving Spirit that extends from Ian's body and outward limitlessly. I can feel the goodness and love that extends outward from his innerness. Then in the next moment I feel this extension mesh with an extension of me and *become* me. Wow, what a magical feeling. Now I have this new insight I can use at any time that allows me to "join" with Ian and see him as me.

RECOGNIZING AUTOMATIC FORGIVENESS

Yesterday, I asked Holy Spirit to help me learn how to be an "automatic forgiver." I want to learn this so I can release the wrong-minded thought instantly. I don't want to carry pain around with me, or regurgitate it later.

When Ian or I have an "ego moment," it helps to minimize the fuss or pain if the other who is connected can remain connected. We have known this for a while. But it has become quite a realization now that the only way to remain connected (and remain in line with the work of the Course) is to remember "what is happening is not real." The ego continues to resurface when it is made real. So, as soon as the pain is initiated and we see the projected error of our wrong mind "straight away" without making it real, and choose Love instead, this is called *automatic forgiveness*. When we do automatic forgiveness, the situation at hand, *known to be false*, is not being fed by wrong-minded thoughts at all and so the correction *must* take place.

THE FUTURE IS NOW?

The future now is recognized as but extension of the present. [WB, pg 457, lesson 314, 1.2] I love this line in today's lesson. I pause as I read it, and then turn my focus to the thought of seeing sinlessness in my brother, in the moment. And that thought extending/projecting into my future. The present, and everything that happens in the now, is a projection that plays on the stage tomorrow. It is important for me to remember this because I have two choices: I can disconnect from my Truth and claim that I or any other is a sinner. Or, I can remain connected and see my brother as sinless and see him as me. If I see another as a sinner, I then project more of the same into the future. When I see "sinning" as an illusion and just a silly mad idea appearing real, then I release the old "ego thoughts of sinning," which can then be removed from my wrong mind.

THAT GENTLE NUDGE

Today, after a telephone call, I was feeling hurt by a friend's remark and started to point the finger. Straight away, Holy

Spirit gently nudged me and whispered to "forgive." Initially, I ignored the nudge and continued to feel hurt. After about 5 minutes of complaining in my mind, I realized I had been "caught" yet again by ego. I had become a victim and had fallen into the trap of seeing two of us, in lieu of one of us.

In the next moment, I receive another gentle nudge reminding me to offer my friend's body to Holy Spirit. I did that. I placed my friend's body in a balloon and asked Holy Spirit to take it. I then felt her true essence that was left. I felt the holy Son of God in my friend. I joined with her as the Sonship. It felt really good to join with her and feel the Oneness.

Once I realized what had happened, and completed my forgiveness lesson, I looked back and recalled the gentle nudge I had received from Holy Spirit. I thanked Holy Spirit for the gentle nudge and reminder. I then told Holy Spirit that I would work at listening to that nudge in the future, so please keep them coming. Yesterday, I prayed to be an automatic forgiver and then today Holy Spirit reminded me, in the moment, to automatically forgive. It feels good to know that Holy Spirit is guiding me every step of the way. I only have to ask to be an automatic forgiver and Holy Spirit will assist me to be one.

FOREVER INNOCENT

In the past few weeks, I have done a number of forgiveness lessons on my back. It is mid October, so it has been about 12 months since my fall. I still carry some residual pain in my lower back; however, it is far less painful than it was a few months ago. I have a feeling these forgiveness lessons are starting to pay off.

When I consider my back and the pain that I made real all of these months, I pause to consider my Truth. If I was able to

194

remember *continually* "who I am" at truth level, then would I have made the pain real to begin with? This question in regards to my Truth is being ignited in me again and again. And that question is, "Who am I?" I am being told that I am the holy Son of God, and I am Love. And I have been shown glimpses of my Truth. But how does this truly feel? Where is that feeling within me? That feeling where I truly *know* I am the holy Son of God?

A feeling tells me I am yet to truly believe that I am the holy Son of God. And until I believe that I am, then I can't possibly "recall what it would feel like." The truth will flow when I open my eyes to the actuality that Truth does indeed reside within me. And that Truth *is* me. So, that is my work now. My work is to constantly remind myself that I *am* the holy Son of God. I am Innocence. I am Abundance. I am Love. I turn to my lesson. Today's Theme of Special Relevance is number **10. What is the Last Judgment?** I read paragraph 5. **This is God's final judgment: "You are still My holy Son, forever innocent, forever loving and forever loved, as limitless as your Creator, and completely changeless and forever pure. Therefore awaken and return to Me. I am your Father and you are My Son."** [WB, pg 455, 5.1]

I WILL NOT HURT MYSELF AGAIN TODAY

Last night Ian and I had a fallout and I was feeling upset with him. Through much effort, I decided to work at doing a forgiveness lesson while I was still feeling very upset. Amazingly, I went from being completely upset to being completely forgivable in less than a minute. Wow! Now *that* was a miracle!

This morning as I begin my lesson, I stop to consider last night and how I did it all to myself. **Lesson 330. I will not hurt myself again today.** [WB, pg 466] There was only one of us in the room, and only one of us disconnected. There was one scared person. And that scared person was me. I was doing it all to myself. Each time I said something to hurt Ian, I was lashing out at myself. Each time he said something to hurt me, it was me fighting with myself. I repeat my lesson. **I will not hurt myself again today.**

I realize today just how important it is to "stop" and do my forgiveness lesson as soon as I disconnect. If I begin to get upset, not only am I re-projecting more of that upset thought, but I am staying stuck in the dream every time I make something real. I want to catch myself and do my forgiveness lessons quickly. No more blaming. No more finger-pointing. No more judging. No more guilt.

Holy Spirit, please make me aware of my oneness with my brother. Please help me to take responsibility and remember that there is only one of us in the room, in the moment. Please help me to remember automatic forgiveness!

I continue on to the first paragraph of my lesson. **Let us this day accept forgiveness as our only function. Why should we attack our minds and give them images of pain?** Today is the day to realize that forgiveness truly is my ONLY function. That is all I need to consider in every moment. I just need to remember that my brother is me. That is the most important thing. If I am upset with my brother then I am upset at myself. If I point the finger at my brother, I am separating instead of joining, and only judging myself. There is only one of us here! One of us to blame...or one of us to love.

FORGIVENESS WORKS!

These past few days I have been thinking a lot about forgiveness and also my truth. They really do go hand in hand. When I believe my truth (that I am the holy Son of God) then I will naturally forgive. How can I begin to make something outside of me real when I already know for a fact that it isn't real? Therefore, instant forgiveness is applied naturally to everything *when I know my truth.*

I just got back from my doctor's appointment where I received MRI results for my back. I was previously told, due to the fall, that even with therapy, it was likely I would have lower back problems for the rest of my life. So, I was speechless when I heard today that my lower back is completely healed. They tell me the slight residual pain that I still feel will decrease to no pain in time. Halleluiah! Of course I grant credit to the forgiveness lessons I have done over the past weeks and feel they are a direct link with this great news. It feels good to know that forgiveness lessons do work! What a miracle! I am not sure how many I was supposed to do; however, a feeling tells me there is no answer. I only need to know that if a separated feeling is forthcoming from my wrong mind then I need to do a forgiveness lesson. Whether I do two or twenty is neither here nor there. I just need to do one every time a wrong-minded thought surfaces.

I feel joy for the faith I have found today in forgiveness lessons. I move forward knowing in my heart now that if I stick with the Course and do the work, then I will remove the blockages to Truth. I sigh at the relief that there *is* light up ahead. And to also come to the realization that miracles will be mine as I continue to forgive wrong-minded thoughts!

FORGET THEIR EGO, JOIN WITH THEIR TRUTH

Today, I felt a friend's anguish and pain relating to a problem that had surfaced in her life. It felt uncomfortable to hear her in pain. As I listened to her, I felt the urge to put her body in a balloon and ask Holy Spirit to take it away. I then felt guided to go beyond her pain and anguish and go to a deeper part of her. As I did that, I began to feel her Truth. As I felt her Truth, I felt her begin to settle down. Following that, a feeling emerged that told me, "Robyn, this is where you can go *all the time* with everyone. You can to go to where their Truth lies."

I felt this shift in my body that is unexplainable. But I felt a major transformation happen within and knew I had been shown the layers of the ego (the depth of our sleep) and how deep I had to go to differentiate between the ego and Truth. I had to give up a lot of levels of ego to get to Truth. But it is there, deep within all of us. And this "Truth" is what I want to communicate with in others. This feeling had come over me that said, "Robyn, when you go directly to the Truth in your brother, you are communicating with your own Truth.

Now I understand that statement, "We all go home together or not at all." If we can't see the Sonship in everyone, then we can't do it on our own. We must "join" to go home. We must remind others of their Truth. In doing so, we remember our own Truth. Only then can we ALL begin to remember who we are...and only then we can all go home.

TO KNOW REALITY

Our world seems to include an ongoing search for happiness. These moments of happiness are what keep us going. They are what make us idolize this dream. Then something happens and our happiness is taken away. So we question and we keep searching because we know there is another answer. We know deep down there *is* something better. But where? We keep looking through the layers of the ego because that is ALL that we know. We search for something else to make us happy. But we soon learn that we have to look elsewhere. We have to go deep. We have to go past the layers of ego. We have to look deep beyond them and deep, deep to where the Sonship still lies. **To know reality is not to see the ego and its** thoughts, its works, its acts, its laws and its beliefs, its dreams, its hopes, its plans for its salvation, and the cost belief in it entails. In suffering, the price for faith in it is so immense that crucifixion of the Son of God is offered daily at its darkened shrine, and blood must flow before the alter where its sickly followers prepare to die. [WB, pg 467, Theme of Special Relevance 12. What is the Ego? 4.1]

The only way to view reality is see the ego as false. But then I have recently said, "Okay, I'll see the Sonship in others instead." Thinking it will be easy. However, as I have come to realize, the layers go very deep. So I ask myself, "How can I see the Sonship when I still see the ego?" I can only see the Sonship when I actually remove the awareness of ego (when I remove the "realness" I have given to ego). I have to make the decision to go deeper than the ego, and go beneath all those layers to the Truth. Then I have to stay there, and speak to that other part of them. I have to learn how to speak to the Sonship.

I really like the last paragraph on that same page in the Workbook. **Yet will one lily of forgiveness change the darkness into light; the altar to illusions to the shrine of Life itself. And peace will be restored forever to the holy minds which God created as His Son, His dwelling place, His joy, His love, completely His, completely one with Him.** [WB, pg 467, 5.1] Hmm, one lily of forgiveness. We know this is quite the journey toward waking up. And the journey is not over in one illusionary day. But it does help to know that just one lily of forgiveness will open the door. I see the work, I see the efforts that lie ahead, and I have opened that door. Every day I am being guided by Holy Spirit. I feel it, and I know it. It took one lily of forgiving and now I am on my way home.

Chapter 21

As I was Created I Remain

FORGIVING OLD PATTERNS

When Holy Spirit bought Ian into my life after handing over the steering wheel, He also bought someone else into my life...Ian's cat, "Cheshire." For as long as I can remember, I had allergic reactions to any type of cat. I would never have dreamed of owning a cat for that reason. So, after returning from Hawaii and moving in with Ian, I at first found Chesh's fur to be somewhat of a problem. Ian did his gentlemanly thing by making sure she didn't get on the sofa or on the bed. However, the fur, still on occasion, bothered me and brought about allergic reactions. I knew, deep down, that this had to be another one of those opportunities to "forgive." So, recently I have been doing some forgiveness lessons on Chesh's fur.

Last week I was doing some exercises. After I finished the exercises I was lying on the floor and Chesh decided to climb onto my stomach, curl up, and take a nap. As I lay there patting her sweet little face, I thought to myself, "Who would have known?" My thoughts immediately returned to the forgiveness lessons I had done in the weeks gone by. I smiled to myself as I realized the allergies I once had when she had come that close to me had miraculously disappeared!

I am sure I will still need to complete more forgiveness lessons; I still run to wash my hands as I am nervous that I might forget and rub my eyes later (this has also led to allergic reactions in the past). So, hopefully, soon I will be rid of any fear when it comes to allergic reactions to cats. However, to know today that I can pat Chesh and have her sit this close to me without any sneezing is still definitely a miracle in itself!

SEEING THE EGO FOR WHAT IT IS

As I notice the ego and understand it better, I can tell ego is everywhere—literally everywhere. I notice the pain, the suffering, the drama, and the questioning. When I see this around me I understand that it is my projection and stuff is coming up for healing; however, I feel at times I am just going round in circles. When I see another that is lost and having difficulty finding their way, I have to realize that person lost is *me,* and they are a projection of how I am feeling. Lately, when I see another creating pain for themselves, I am beginning to take responsibility by saying, "I am doing this to myself." I am learning to forgive. If I see an alcoholic, I see it is a part of *my* wrong mind. I see that person is me doing it to myself. I am starting to recognize *my* wrong mind projecting out there in so many different ways.

In Ian's and my relationship, I see us appeasing each other's ego. We "try" to make each other's ego happy. That is what we have both been good at for a very long time. Ego taught us to appease it from an early age, in an effort to "try" to make everybody happy. An ego world it truly is. I am beginning to see it as that.

When we appease each other, does it "heal" the thing that bothered us? No. The projection on the problem as we try to appease and fix it only projects it yet again. And then we turn around only to appease it again next time it surfaces.

And then I think I am doing well and a great student of the Course. But at the end of the day, I am ego, believing that I can wake-up, and believing that I am a good Course student. So there I go pleasing myself by telling myself what a good student I am! The ego paints itself pretty. When we appease it and make it happy, it smiles and then we smile. And then everything is okay until we have to appease it again.

I did a forgiveness lesson before on appeasing the ego. I saw the appeasing thought illusionary and part of my wrong mind. I then asked Holy Spirit to take that thought and I chose Love instead. It is interesting as I come to the realization that when I am appeasing the ego in another it is really me appeasing *myself!*

ALL I GIVE I GIVE TO MYSELF

I have pondered the title of this book for a while now. Last night I told Ian I could see the word "miracle" in the title. Ian said he could see the word "forgiveness" in the title. Following our conversation, a feeling came over me that said, "Pay attention tomorrow when you do your lesson."

This morning, I am relaxing on the patio and doing my lesson and reading the Theme of Special Relevance number **13. What is a Miracle?** As I read the line **Forgiveness is the home of miracles** [WB, pg 473, 3.1] my body perks up and I feel this "yes" surface from within. I have no hesitation that I am being guided to this line in the Course to make it the title of this book.

I continue to do my lesson. **Lesson 343. I am not asked to make a sacrifice to find the mercy and the peace of God.** [WB, pg 475] I read on to paragraph 2.2. **Salvation has no cost. It is a gift that must be freely given and received.** It doesn't cost me to remember who I am. And it doesn't cost me to remember, "all I give I give to myself." Also, to remember that salvation is my "return to memory of Truth." It can only cost me if I continue to choose to see the ego in myself. No, I am not asked to make a sacrifice to find the mercy and the peace of God. I sacrifice nothing. I can only gain, for God only gives, and what God gives is all I wish to remember.

The good news is that I am catching myself re-projecting egoic thoughts. I am now catching myself choosing to be separate. I choose the separation when I believe my brother is doing something to me. I still choose to separate much of the day. And each time I do, I close the lid on God. I block out the Light. I choose the dark...again. And then I choose to be in the dark again tomorrow.

WHAT I GIVE MY BROTHER IS MY GIFT TO ME

I am beginning to trust that there is only ONE of us. Every time I judge my brother I am judging myself. Every time I forgive my brother I am forgiving myself. I don't want to drag this on any longer. I want to take off these chains that bind me to the darkness. I want to remember in every instant that I am doing EVERYTHING to myself! I no longer *choose* to see my brother as outside of me. What a miracle. **Miracles fall like drops of healing rain from Heaven on a dry and dusty world, where starved and thirsty creatures come to die. Now they have water. Now the world is green. And everywhere the signs of**

life spring up, to show that what is born can never die, for what has life has immortality. [WB, Theme of Special Relevance 13. What is a Miracle? pg 473, 5.1]

Lesson 344. Today I learn the law of love; that what I give my brother is my gift to me. [WB, pg 475] The more I focus on today's lesson, the more I realize that my own love is in my own hands. If I wish to feel love, I must BE love. I am in control of *how I feel* all the time. Every time I join with my brother it is a gift I am giving MYSELF. It is entirely up to me how I want to feel in every moment. If I separate from my brother, I WILL feel the separation—that yucky feeling within. If I join with my brother, I will feel the love—that yummy feeling within. I gift myself and my brother every time I join.

ANOTHER ROAD TRIP

This weekend was Thanksgiving. Ian and I drove up the coastal route of California to Half Moon Bay. The coastal scenery along the way was breathtaking. We stayed overnight at Half Moon Bay, and in the evening we visited the local "Moss Beach Distillery" where we enjoyed a delicious Thanksgiving dinner. It was really nice to relax and enjoy the view over the Pacific, and spend some quality time together. The waiter told us some stories about the Moss Beach Distillery and how it became famous for its ghost inhabitants. We both glanced around the restaurant half expecting to see a ghost or two—but not a ghost in sight. Hey, maybe they went home for Thanksgiving!

The next morning, we woke up early to the start of a crisp, cool day. We weren't sure if we were going to stay around the area or head north. So we studied a map and jointly made a decision to jump in the car and head further north to Napa Valley. It was a beautiful drive through San Francisco and over the golden gate bridge. The early morning traffic was busy through San Francisco, and as we sat in the traffic I took in some of my favorite features of this city—the lovely, old, Victorian style homes.

As we drove into Napa Valley, the vineyards painted the landscape in brilliant reds, oranges, and browns. It was breathtaking scenery. We visited a few wineries and had a great day hanging out in the valley. We were pleased with our decision to venture up this way. It was a really nice time. The following day, unfortunately, we needed to get back to business in LA.

The whole trip was enjoyable and we both appreciated the relaxing break from the busy city life back in LA. Escaping on a country road trip seems to be the perfect antidote to city life for both of us.

MIRACLES MIRROR GOD'S ETERNAL LOVE

Recently, it is becoming clearer why I need to forgive. However, am I truly ready to release the ego's ways? That's the question. How ready am I to see Ian and others as myself? And then beyond that, how ready am I to believe that there is something better on the other side—where Light resides? **Lesson 350. Miracles mirror God's eternal Love. To offer them is to remember Him, and through His memory to save the world.** [WB, pg 478] How ready am I to choose miracles and to play my part in saving the world? Am I ready to make that decision? Am I ready to truly walk away from this dream and rid of everything I have ever known? Am I ready to believe I am so much more than ego? Am I ready to stand up and say I am the *holy Son of God?*

This feeling comes over me that says, "Accept the *real* you! It's time. You know the answers, Robyn. Now, it's up to you."

I must believe that happiness will be mine when I forgive. I have to believe in Holy Spirit. I have to hand over the wheel entirely. I am not that good—not yet. I take the wheel back. I take control and I judge prior to forgiving. I have to STOP taking the wheel back. Every time I take it back, I am saying "yes" to ego and "no" to forgiveness lessons.

It is like a double edged sword at times. I swap between Truth and ego. I choose Holy Spirit one minute, then I fall right back into the dream state and choose the clutches of the ego in the next.

I find myself at times wondering if forgiveness lessons really do work. But recently I have been getting verification that they do. I have to learn to trust forgiveness lessons. I do feel in my heart when I can trust them one hundred percent they will always work for me. Faith is so important when doing this work.

I pause to repeat my lesson. **Lesson 350.** I read the first line in the first paragraph. ***What we forgive becomes a part of us, as we perceive ourselves.*** So as I forgive I offer the opportunity of joining and in that instant I set my brother and myself free...to stand united as we were created. There is only ONE of us. I must drum that into myself. Remembering that my brother is me will help me to forgive.

So, I must remember, firstly, that my brother is me. Then, secondly, do a forgiveness lesson. And, thirdly, have faith in forgiveness lessons. They do work!

Ian and I have talked about the one thing that continues to regurgitate between us. We are each afraid of upsetting the other person and on the flip side we are each afraid of being hurt. Hmm, so, fear of hurting the other versus fear of being hurt. At some level we don't want to hurt each other because we seem to know that we are joined. But then the fear is

206

greater. Out of fear we are protecting ourselves from either getting into trouble or from dealing with a sore heart. It's all about self-protection really. But that is how the ego works. Day one, the ego went into self-protection mode when it/we feared God. To this day, as the ego, we have been going around the hamster wheel doing the same thing over and over and over. We are only just beginning to see the Light outside of the hamster wheel. Yet, it is so unknowing. What do we know really? Only what we have known for lifetimes. It is blind faith. All we have is this gentle little Voice inside of our heads that says, "Come this way. Come with me, I'll show you the way." The faith we need to get off that wheel forever is clearer than it has ever been to me. In other words, the faith we need to hand over the wheel entirely to Holy Spirit is tenfold of what I ever imagined. No wonder we have run around the hamster wheel for so long—for so many lifetimes. No wonder it is difficult to choose Love over fear.

As I complete lesson 350, I realize we all need miracles in our lives. Miracles reveal God's Love to us. The whole "accepting," "letting go," and then "joining" comes from forgiveness. That is the Miracle. That is the essence of God's Love.

MY SINLESS BROTHER IS MY GUIDE TO PEACE

Today's lesson is **Lesson 351. My sinless brother is my guide to peace. My sinful brother is my guide to pain. And which I choose to see I will behold.** [WB, pg 480] I read on. *Who is my brother but your holy Son? And if I see him sinful I proclaim myself a sinner, not a Son of God; alone and friendless in a fearful world.* I stop to consider the meaning of this. For my whole life I believed that everyone was outside of me. And lately, Holy Spirit is working through me to see my brother as myself. While I keep my brother separate from me means that I can still be hurt, and I will still judge. It also means that pain will continue. If I want true peace then I have to see that my brother is me. This morning I sat here saying over and over, "My brother is me," "My brother is me," "My brother is me." I HAVE to get this. I have no other choice. I have to STOP separating. I have to stop judging. I have to stop making the dream real. I have to stop making the ego real. I struggle with it. I struggle with the fact that no one is doing anything outside of me. But I have to know that I can't struggle any longer!

There is no other alternative if I wish to remember my true identity and go home. *I have to stop making anything and everything around me real!*

BETWEEN TWO WORLDS

I was telling Ian yesterday I feel as though I am in between two worlds right now. It's almost like I have one foot in one world (wrong mind) and the other foot in the other world (Right Mind). I guess I just have to take that leap of faith and leave wrong mind behind. As I consider the meaning of leaving the wrong mind completely behind, it feels like I almost have to lose respect for the things I have been taught to respect. And like I can no longer care as I have been taught to care. The thought of that still scares me.

I turn to today's lesson. **Lesson 355. There is no end to all the peace and joy, and all the miracles that I will give, when I accept God's word. Why not today?** [WB, pg 482] I read on. *Why should I wait, my Father, for the joy You promised me? For You will keep Your Word You have Your Son in exile. I am sure my treasure waits for me, and I need but reach out my hand to find it. Even now my fingers touch it. It is very close. I need not wait an instant more to be at peace forever.* It is amazing how I feel in between the two worlds and today's lesson is urging me to take that extra step. It is urging me to go to where my treasure awaits me.

It feels so good to know I am this close. I have come this far—where the Right Mind awaits my entry. Holy Spirit holds out his hand and beckons me. I feel the beckoning. I do feel it is better where I am heading. But then a part of me has fear in picking up that last foot that is still on the side of wrong mind. I guess I have to be patient and stay put and not allow my fears to pull me back because I feel they could pull me right back at any time. A feeling tells me I just have to be patient and await my readiness and Holy Spirit will assist me.

Today, I focus on welcoming God. I feel Holy Spirit's presence continually now and expect his answer each time I ask. It is never too far away. The feelings of the hurdles up ahead, which I must move beyond, come with the sincere confirmation that I will never be alone. I feel the tingles of laughter and joy that I will encounter along the way. I feel Holy Spirit's gentle push and encouragement.

THE FINAL LESSONS

Lesson 361 to 365. This holy instant would I give to You. Be You in charge. For I would follow You, certain that Your direction gives me peace. [WB, pg 486] The final lesson comes close to my heart. As I look back over the past year and a half, I have found my connection with Holy Spirit to be one of the most important factors...if not the most important of my entire journey. If I wasn't able to feel the presence of Holy Spirit and have faith that He is guiding me, then I would be completely lost. I am thankful for the guidance and love that I have recognized daily from Holy Spirit. And I am thankful to Jesus for reminding me throughout the lessons of my Eternal Guidance. I want to take this final lesson with me every day for the rest of my life. If I will always be aware of Holy Spirit's presence, I know I will always find my way.

His is the only way to find the peace that God has given us. It is His way that everyone must travel in the end, because it is this ending God Himself appointed. [WB, pg 485, Final Lessons - Introduction, 2.1]

This Course is a beginning, not an end. Your Friend goes with you. You are not alone. No one who calls on Him can call in vain. Whatever troubles you, be certain that He has the answer, and will gladly give it to you, if you simply turn to Him and ask it of Him. He will not withhold all answers that you need for anything that seems to trouble you. He knows the way to solve all problems, and resolve all doubts. His certainty is yours. You need but ask it of Him, and it will be given you. [WB, Epilogue, pg 487, 1.1]

"Holy Spirit, I won't forget You now. I walk with You, hand in hand, and know that through You I will remember Who I Am and Who my Father Is. Thank You. Amen."

Chapter 22

In Paradise with God

LOOKING BACK BUT MOVING FORWARD

Here I am back in my favorite place in the whole world. Can you guess where it is? Looking over my shoulder while I write this, Ian says, "In his arms." How cute. Well yes, that too. So, after finishing my lessons and sharing my journey with you, I figured I couldn't leave you at home. I thought I would bring you to Hawaii with me...just one more time!

We have rented a lovely home in Punalu'u. Punalu'u is a picturesque spot on the North Eastern Coast of Oahu. It is quiet and serene, and we just love it here. The view from our vacation home reveals majestic, rolling mountains and a beautiful manicured yard that overlooks a private beach and turquoise waters. Occasionally, we see rainbows overhead, and below we catch glimpses of a neighboring peacock wandering by. This morning, we sit on our large wraparound lanai taking in all of this. Can it get any better? This gentle knowing Voice from within says, "Yes Robyn, it gets so much better." Okay, I say. Sign me up!

As Christmas Carols play in the background, Ian is cooking up some breakfast, and I smile to myself while thinking how happy I am to be sharing this special time of the year in Hawaii with him. I think of the reason for our time away and celebrating. It is Jesus' birthday. I pause to give thanks to Jesus for "A Course in Miracles" and the Workbook lessons that assist me in learning how to forgive and go home.

SHARING THE JOURNEY

I have decided it might be fun to add a final chapter to the book by looking back over the past year, with Ian and I discussing what we have each learned along the way—from a Course student perspective, and also from a non-Course student perspective. Ian agrees to play along. While we sit here eating a yummy breaky and enjoying paradise on our lanai, we get a feeling that this would be the perfect time to start. We begin by discussing our flight over from LA yesterday...

Robyn: There was quite a different energy between us yesterday in our travelling together, don't you think?
Ian: Yeah, I noticed that too. I was feeling stressed yesterday. I was so wrapped up in wanting to get on the plane quickly to get room for our overhead luggage. And I was thinking if they didn't fit then we would have to "check" our bags. And if they checked our bags, then we might not get out in time to get our rental car from the airport. It worried me that our flight got in so late, and that we only had 15 minutes before the rental car place closed. So I was concerned that we might get stuck at the airport for 5 or 6 hours. And I was just so wrapped up in all of that. I was worried that our arrival in Hawaii wouldn't go smoothly.

Robyn: When we were having lunch at LAX and you mentioned your concerns, I felt that worrying wasn't going to help us get to the rental car in time. We just had to go with what was going to unfold.

Ian: Well, that's the difference between you and me. You have the faith and I don't in situations like that. I have to think about things. I have to plan things. I don't feel that something out there is guiding me. I feel it's up to me to determine how things unfold.

Robyn: As you go about your day do you feel that you are on your own?

Ian: There are those times, those brief moments, when everything seems right and everything seems to align. Those times when you feel at peace and joyous and everything seems great.

Robyn: Hmm...do you know why you couldn't feel that way yesterday?

Ian: I guess if I'm not preoccupied or worried about something, then maybe that is the time I can relax and focus with clarity. But there is no way that feeling can come in if I am on a trip or involved in business—that wouldn't happen. Because I believe unless I control the steps and the outcome then it's not going to turn out the way I want it to. So letting go of the steering wheel and stop worrying about stuff is the thing to do.

Robyn: Right, I understand. From a young age we are taught to control things.

Ian: Yeah, and that's why I think about the overhead stuff. I feel that I have to control it.

Robyn: Yeah and that's the difference. We are either controlling it, or we are handing over the wheel.

Ian: Yeah, and I hate it.

Robyn: I hate it too. I know when I do that. When I want you to be a certain way, or tell me certain things; like a way that will make me happy and feel good. I don't want to feel that I need to control it. I want to know that I can trust. I think there are different reasons why we don't trust at times. There are certain things that I am going to control through ego. And there are certain things that you are going to control.

Ian: I watch you on a daily basis. I think you let go of the steering wheel a lot.

Robyn: Well, I still need to be aware. I know I still take it back a lot too.

Ian: You don't fret. My sister tells me that I am too tense, and too uptight.

Robyn: Well, you are more relaxed now than you were. I can see that.

Ian: You could tell last night going on the trip how tense I got. You felt it before we even left the house.

Robyn: Yeah, I could tell as soon as we left the house. I thought to myself, "Okay, it's time to give Ian his space for a while." (chuckle) But I also knew that as soon as we got on the plane and got seated that you would feel okay and then you would relax. I think it's part of that journey thing. Are we able to enjoy the moment? I do the same thing at times. I want to hurry and get everything done so I can sit back and relax.

Ian: You know, if I travel on my own, then I am more okay. When I am with you, I feel I want to take care of you as well. Like when you got stopped with your bags. I want to protect you from that. I don't want you to go through that.

Robyn: But you see I took it as though you were annoyed with me and frustrated because of me.

Ian: Well, that was a hassle. I don't want you to go through that.

Robyn: But I wasn't even bothered. I only had to put my handbag in another bag. It didn't bother me at all.

Ian: Yeah, but we got separated. And I didn't like that. I didn't like not being able to fix it. I feel like everything that goes wrong I have to fix it.

Robyn: Yeah, I understand. But you're not responsible.

Ian: I like taking care of you though. It's what we are taught when we are growing up as young men. We are taught to open the door for the lady and take care of her at dinner.

Robyn: Yeah, but behind all of this something is coming up for healing. Like with that bag situation. I start to get stressed also because I feel your anxiety. Then I think to myself, "What's the big deal?" And then I think, "It is difficult traveling with him right now. Why can't he just relax? Why does this need to be a big deal?" There you go. There is the lesson.

Ian: Yeah, there is a big lesson in that.

Robyn: Yeah, for me, a big fat forgiveness lesson!

Ian: I wasn't concerned about you getting stressed with the bags because you're not that type of person. But I just wanted everything to go smoothly for you. I should have just said, "Take as many bags as you like. Do whatever you like."

Robyn: Yeah. Like, take 20 bags, but you're carrying them yourself. (chuckle)

Ian: But the fact of the matter is that I want everything to go smoothly. Then I see problems here and problems there.

Robyn: But isn't it funny how I didn't see any problems.

Ian: But see the bottom line is I'm a control freak.

Robyn: Yeah, I told you that when I met you (chuckle). But then, see! Me judging you instead of forgiving that will cause it to continue to resurface in our relationship. I have to forgive it. I have to realize that I am you, and I am the control freak too. That is part of MY wrong mind. The one wrong mind. I am judging you when I get upset with you and your anxiousness in wanting my bags to be fine. You may have initially wanted to control and judge it...

Ian: I didn't judge it.

Robyn: Well...don't you think wanting to control something stems from a judgment?

Ian: Ah, maybe...yeah.

Robyn: So, instead of *me* doing my forgiveness lesson, I end up judging in the moment. So in me judging you in the moment means we are getting stuck in the physical world—in the dream—and we can't heal. While I am judging you, we just can't heal.

Ian: So it is self perpetuating. Unless we realize that what we are doing is coming from wrong mind.

Robyn: Isn't it weird? And there is *one* of us doing it. So then I want to ask myself, "Why am witnessing it?" I could be wrong, but I don't think you can witness anything that you haven't judged prior to it manifesting.

Ian: You can't witness anything that you haven't judged? Hmm, so you can't see anything that you haven't cast an opinion on?

Robyn: Yeah. Like, for example, looking back to being a child in trouble. The child who got hit by a parent is saying, "I don't like him. He's mean to me. My bottom is stinging right now." Isn't that a judgment coming from the child? Whether we like it or not, that is part of the ego mind that is being passed on continually. It is part of the wrong mind being activated, or a judgment being activated.

Ian: So, the end goal is—or the answer is—to get out of that mindset. But don't you then get accused of being blasé and not caring?

Robyn: Yeah, I guess.

Ian: So, let's look at last night with the bag situation. So, theoretically I should have just gone up the escalator and not worried and just left you there. (chuckle)

Robyn: Well, you kind of did. And you were good with that. But I could still feel your stress from the bottom of the escalator. Or, my own stress I should say...since I am you.

Ian: Well, it's good that I did. Otherwise I would have gotten in an argument with that lady.

Robyn: Really? But did you see the nice conversation I was having with her? I just didn't want to squash your Christmas pressie's honey by putting my handbag on top of them. I told her that and she was sweet about it.

Ian: Well, following that, we had good luck at the next security stop where they x-rayed our bags! Remember we were walking toward that long line of people when suddenly a door opened to our left and a guy diverted us. He ushered us into that x-ray room and we were the first people to enter it. We bypassed a lot of people up ahead that were waiting to go

216

through that *other* x-ray section. That was great! No-one in front us of us!

Robyn: Yeah. And didn't we say that everything unfolds for a reason?

Ian: So, if you weren't stopped with your bags, then we would have been waiting in that long line!

Robyn: Right. So, isn't that interesting how everything happens for a reason? And when we see that...

Ian: Yes, see that, and stop worrying about the moment in time, and know that it's okay, it's all good...

Robyn: And what time did we get to the house last night?

Ian: 1am.

Robyn: Earlier than we expected ha.

Ian: It's funny. I think Conrad (the caretaker of the home) is very spiritual. Did you hear him when he was trying to open the front door for us and had trouble with it?

Robyn: I wasn't really paying attention. I was excited and looking around. I could tell though that he was half asleep.

Ian: He was really chilled and said, "It's okay, it's okay." He was fine. He wasn't stressed at all. And he must have been tired at that time of the morning. I was saying to myself, "Come on. Get the bloody door open."

Robyn: But you were tired honey. No wonder. You wiped yourself out with all that worrying. (chuckle)

Ian: It was fricken exhausting. Hey, maybe that's why I'm always tired!

Robyn: Well, look at how well everything worked out. Whether we worried or not it was going to work out that way.

Ian: Yeah, so true. Hey, let's go for a drive and check out the North Shore, and maybe go for a snorkel?

Robyn: Sounds good to me!

LATER THAT DAY

Ian: Today while driving, I got to thinking about our conversation this morning, and you know...if I stop and sit down for a minute and think about what you have said before...that everything has already happened...

<u>Robyn</u>: Right, because time is an illusion...

<u>Ian</u>: Right. If you adopt that philosophy, then every minute of every day, you would never worry about anything because it has already happened. We are just living it out. So, what's the point in worrying about anything? But what if you run over some dude and kill him, then what? And you walk away thinking it was going to happen anyway and say, "Sorry dude, it wasn't me. It was going to happen." But seriously, imagine that! You would have people walking through life not giving a shit about anything!

<u>Robyn</u>: Well, you *would* be perceived as though you don't care.

<u>Ian</u>: Yeah. "Hey, it wasn't me, it was pre-destined." But doesn't that give you an out-card for everything? Like for responsibility?

<u>Robyn</u>: There are two ways to look at that. Like the puppy dog that we saw killed on the road earlier. You could be someone that walks away and couldn't care less. Or you might be someone that says, "I know that everything happens for a reason so I have to be okay with this."

<u>Ian</u>: But when you say that everything has already happened, then why would we do anything? Why would we care about anything? Why not put our feet up, relax, and just let the world go by?

<u>Robyn</u>: Well, everything has already happened because time is an illusion. But, right now, we still have to get to where we are going because it IS happening right now within the dream. But because time is an illusion then in essence it has already happened. It can sound confusing, and bizarre, but yeah, we still have to walk this path. So, you can say, "I'm not going to care or I am not going to do anything." Or you can say, "I do care, so I'm going to trust and listen for guidance and then take the guided steps."

Ian: I think there are people that may take solace in the Course and shed responsibility in their own life, and believe that they can let go and not think anymore.

Robyn: You can't be too blasé that you don't really care. You have to see that there is an end result you are striving for. And you've got to have a lot of faith. It's like what we've said before, "There is something else going on here and there is someone else guiding us to peace and on to a good outcome." But we must follow that guidance.

Ian: But you still don't relinquish control of your own life right?

Robyn: As far as the path we take...it is up to us if we want to control how things unfold along the way. We can hand over the wheel and listen to guidance, or we can hold the wheel firmly and ignore any guidance. We have free will. However, the outcome *is* certain. We *will* wake-up....because it has already happened. However, the decisions we make today and tomorrow *do* matter because they are the decisions that take us *toward* waking up *within the dream*.

Ian: But how can it matter when everything has already happened?

Robyn: It matters because even though it has already happened you are just taking away time. You are not taking away what is happening *now* within the dreamscape of waking up.

Ian: So what you are saying is that even though the events in our life have already happened, not everything is pre-ordained and we still control the destiny of where we are heading?

Robyn: We can control it if we wish and that will only keep us stuck in the dream. Or, we can be guided by Holy Spirit to wake up, and that will set us free. When we receive the guidance, then the decision is ultimately our own in *choosing* to listen to that guidance. We can either stay asleep and keep going around in circles dreaming this dream of being in an ego body, or we could see that there is something greater about ourselves that we have forgotten and work toward remembering that. Either way, it is a timeless passing. Time is an illusion...and we have already woken up. *But* in the dream-world of time we are still yet to make that decision.

Ian: Hey, do you see something bobbing up and down on the water out there?

Robyn: Yeah, is it a turtle? Or, maybe a coconut?

Ian: It may very well be a coconut. It is just bobbing around. It is either that, or a very lazy turtle who's realized that life has already happened, so he is just bobbing around anyway. (chuckle)

Robyn: (chuckling) That's funny.

(Pause)

(While looking out at the turquoise waters) You know, I really love it here. Look at all those colors in the water.

Ian: Yeah, me too. (pause) I think you're right...it's a coconut going with the tide. Okay, let's pause this recording...

Robyn: Yeah, let's go for a walk.

IT IS HIS WAY EVERYONE MUST TRAVEL IN THE END

(A rainy morning...we're sitting on the lanai watching the water change colors with the passing clouds and frequent showers...an enjoyable picture)

Ian: So how long did it take you to complete the lessons in the Workbook?

Robyn: Hmm, well I started July last year. So...about 17 months.

Ian: You know, I don't think there should be a time stamp on it.

Robyn: Well...I think it is meant to be what feels right to you. Remember that time in Lanikai when I did that lesson for about a week? I kept getting the feeling to repeat it.

Ian: Yeah, I do.

Robyn: And then sometimes I would think that I didn't do a lesson right, and the next morning I would wake up and get a feeling to go on to the next lesson, and that always surprised me when that happened. Now, at the end of the lessons, the most important thing I have learned is we can't find our way on our own. We must be guided out of this dream. And if we think we can find our own way, then we will get lost. That guidance from within is really the most important part of this whole journey. I really like that part in the introduction to the final lessons: **His is the only way to find the peace that God has given us. It is His way that everyone must travel in the end. Because it is this ending that God Himself appointed.** [WB, pg 485, 2.1] So, the only way to find home is to follow Holy Spirit and follow His Intention and Knowledge.

Ian: It could have been a shorter book really couldn't it? (chuckles)

Robyn: Yeah. (chuckling) It could have just said, "Follow Holy Spirit and do your forgiveness lessons."

Ian: It took her 7 years to dictate the message. All that was really needed was that one sentence.

Robyn: To complete the whole book? Helen Schucman?

Ian: Yeah. (pause) I guess the whole point of the Course's message is that you know nothing. You are starting from scratch.

Robyn: Yeah, it seems easy and straight forward, but to implement the steps of the Course is a whole other story. (pause) Hey, remember when I was in Lanikai and I was interested in learning how to do forgiveness lessons? Then right when I got back from Lanikai we were getting on really well, but not long after we started butting heads a bit. Then as we butt heads more and more we both wanted harmony. It was around that time that I became very serious about doing forgiveness lessons. And soon after, I was guided to more clarity and then those steps in forgiveness.

Ian: Yeah, I recall that day as we drove across Alligator Alley in Florida and we talked about the steps in doing forgiveness lessons. It was all about choosing Right Mind over wrong mind.

Robyn: I needed steps that resonated with me. And I needed forgiveness lessons that resonated with me. I think anyone can tell you how to do a forgiveness lesson but you have to be ready and willing to do them. And then on top of that, believe in them. It's getting to that point where you *know* in your heart what a forgiveness lesson is and you *know* it is going to work for you.

Ian: I like your thing about putting the subject/person in a bubble or a balloon and letting it go.

Robyn: Yeah, that was Gary's. I got that from his last seminar. I like that too.

Ian: It is cool watching it drift off. That helps. (pause) So, what now?

Robyn: So, today, I always seek to join with you and others and forgive wrong-minded thinking.

Ian: Yeah, I know you are. I can tell you are. But what about the lessons? Now that you have finished them don't you feel like you are losing a teacher—something to fall back on— something that gives you some sanity through all of this?

Robyn: Yeah, it does feel kind of scary.

Ian: Yeah, I am sure it is. Because if we butt heads you run off and do your lesson. But now you don't have that.

Robyn: Well, what I am going to do now is my "forgiveness lessons." The last lesson in the Workbook reminds me that Holy Spirit is always there for me, and will always hear me and answer me. So I have to remember that I'm never alone. And now I have to really put into practice everything I've learned.

Ian: That's the tricky part because now it's not in your face every day. It's like at school, when you have exams, and then you leave school, and you end up forgetting so much of what you learned because it's not in your face anymore.

Robyn: Yeah, you're right. So, now I have to make that decision...to make this a part of my life every day. You know what will help me to remember?

Ian: What?

Robyn: When we have fallouts. Because I want peace. I want to feel good with you. And I want to feel good with others. And that right there will make me want to do my forgiveness lessons. I want to feel peace with us. That is important to me.

If we continue to judge each other, the ego prevails. I don't want that, because I know that's not the answer.

Ian: Well, you know it's going to be tough.

Robyn: Yeah. Every day I am going to have to be *aware*. Awareness is like gold. I have to be aware so I can do my forgiveness lessons.

Ian: Do you ever think you will go back to the lessons? I don't mean to do them, but referencing back to them?

Robyn: Yeah, for sure. I think of ones that have impacted me often. Remember at Ken Wapnick's seminar? He referenced lessons at times.

Ian: Oh, yeah.

Robyn: I don't think there is any right or wrong. That's the whole point of all this. What are you being guided to? What is Holy Spirit telling you right now? We have to stop judging and trying to control things. And we have to listen and trust that Voice.

Ian: How different do you feel from this time last year?

Robyn: I feel more aware. When I started doing the lessons I feel that...

Ian: But not much bothered you when you were doing PF1. You created harmony in your life. But now you are dealing with a lot more stuff. You are dealing with discontentment.

Robyn: Yes, that's true. And that is a big shift. I think you have to believe in yourself and know that you can do this. It isn't easy at times. You have to believe in yourself as the Sonship and not as the ego. So, now that I have finished the lessons, each morning I will spend some time joining with Holy Spirit. I will hand over the wheel in the morning and ask Holy Spirit to guide me through the day. And I am going to work at becoming more and more aware of Holy Spirit's presence and guidance throughout the day.

Ian: It's funny isn't it? All you're really asking for is to be aware.

Robyn: Yeah. Hmm, well, what is awareness?

Ian: It's tapping into what you already know.

Robyn: Yeah, tapping into what you already know. I like that.

Ian: You know what...I don't care that it has been raining a lot on this trip.

Robyn: Yeah. It doesn't matter...the view is incredible whether it's sunny or raining. You look this way and see huge mountains which look awesome with the mistiness and hovering rainbows...and you look that way and see the ocean which changes color as the weather changes.

Ian: The East Coast offers all of this. Hey, I read earlier that Punalu'u means "coral dived for."

Robyn: Really. That makes sense. There is coral reef all along the coast line here. (pause) So what's your favorite thing about being here?

Ian: I like the tranquility. I like the fact that there are no people around.

Robyn: (giggles) No ego's around.

Ian: You don't feel the stress of the normal day to day crap.

Robyn: When you think about it, we have to be careful not to segregate ourselves. There is learning to do. Forgiveness lessons to do. Not that we don't get enough from each other. (giggles)

Ian: Why can't we be like the Buddhists?

Robyn: Well, I guess there must be a way to wake up like that—connecting with Spirit continually. I'm sure there is. But this is Jesus' way. Getting amongst the people.

Ian: You could never get away from the ego unless you live on a desert island. And this place is overpopulated. I don't know how they qualify overpopulation. I guess too many people to deal with the lack of natural resources. You know, I keep thinking about how we are going to be when we live here. How we are going to feel. I have heard many people speak of island fever and after a time they feel the urge to move back to the mainland and revert back to a more conventional lifestyle. What are your thoughts on that?

Robyn: Well, I feel that we are both able to "be" with ourselves, and neither of us require outside stimulation so much. So I don't know if I see us getting bored and seeking that faster pace lifestyle, or reverting back to the lifestyle that we currently have in California.

Ian: Yeah, I agree. The lifestyle here would be a chance for us to explore our inner journeys further without the "white noise," or in other words, the distraction of everyday life.

Robyn: Yeah. And I would say that if the move feels right at the time then it will most likely be a good thing. We just have to "listen" to the way we feel within, and follow that. If it is meant to be, then we will know.

Ian: Right now a move here feels good, however, the crunch time will come when we are faced with making that ultimate decision, and at that time I have no doubt I will feel guided to make the right decision.

Robyn: You know...last night, it was cool hearing the lapping of those waves on the beach as we were falling asleep. And then you said, "What's that other noise?" And we realized that it was larger waves crashing on the reef out further. So we heard the soft waves lapping and the larger waves crashing at the same time. That was really cool ha?

Ian: Yeah, that was cool.

Robyn: I remember what the most upsetting thing for me was when I found out this was a dream. I always loved the beach and the water. I was so upset when I found out that it wasn't real. I remember asking Ken Wapnick, "What do I do now when I go to the beach? Can I still enjoy it?"

Ian: What did he say?

Robyn: He told me to enjoy it but just know in the back of my mind that it isn't real. Then the next week I went to the beach and tried to see it like he said. I worked at that.

Ian: That goes for everything. Remember that conversation when you were in Hawaii-Kai and I was in California, and you said you have to acknowledge that this is a dream. Do you remember that?

Robyn: Yeah, that was one of those steps that I took. I was asking to wake up and see it as a dream, even though I already knew that it was a dream...well believed that it was. At that point I finally realized that I wanted to start leaving the dream.

225

Ian: And you were concerned as you didn't know what the consequences were?

Robyn: Yeah, well I didn't want to leave *you*.

Ian: Right.

Robyn: That was the hard part. But now I have come to terms with the fact that I want to leave the dream.

Ian: Well that fear that you had was unfounded.

Robyn: True. I see now that you are coming with me.

Ian: I call that the separation as you saw me as outside of you and where you were going.

Robyn: Yeah, I was concerned.

Ian: And I was concerned.

Robyn: See, that shows us how this gentle shift is happening, because we don't have those feelings today. But is there a major shift between back then and now? No. It has just been a gentle shift that has happened. We could sit here right now and say, "I am not afraid of leaving the dream anymore because you're coming with me."

Ian: Well everything is.

Robyn: Yeah, everything will. But at that time you were the focal point in that. It was more about you. I was afraid of leaving you. I had already gone through leaving other people, like family and friends, and then other stuff too...remember about the beach.

Ian: Believe me I thought it was about me as well.

Robyn: What makes you say that?

Ian: Well it was like you had a bus ticket somewhere and I didn't have one!

Robyn: (laughing) Oh, honey I wasn't going to get on the bus without you. (Pause) (still laughing). Right now I'm kind of on the bus, and you've got one foot on the step of the bus and one foot on the road. You're like, "Should I really pick up this big book? This 1,200 plus page book!"

Ian: It's like, "Should I get on the bus or not?"

Robyn: And you're really not sure ha. You don't know if you'll do the lessons.

Ian: It's not like I'm not sure...It's like I'm...(pause)

Robyn: not sure. (chuckling)

Ian: No, I don't think about it. I am waiting for when it feels right.

Robyn: Well, that's good that you're listening to that guidance.

Ian: I have never been one to dive in to something. I'm intrigued and through you I'm learning a lot. But am I at that stage when I am going to do the lessons? I don't know. (pause) Maybe I'm just being lazy. Maybe I'll just let you do the work and learn through you.

Robyn: Yeah, ride on my coattails. (chuckle) I remember I was doing the lessons when we first met. I was what, 6 months into the lessons when we started dating. You really had zero knowledge of the Course at the time. But something said to me that that was okay. And to just keep doing what I was doing. I recall not really talking to you about it. I was doing the lessons for months and we didn't really talk about it.

Ian: I recall you saying that it wasn't really religious. You know, I always remember watching that program where Jerry Jampolsky said that he was concerned that his friends would think he was a "God freak" or a "Jesus freak." You can't deny it is a type of religion.

Robyn: Well, what is religion to you?

Ian: I have a bad view of religion.

Robyn: But, what is religion to you?

Ian: What do you mean? What is my opinion of it?

Robyn: I think it is a good idea to ask yourself what is religion to you, and then what is ACIM to you? Then to look at both of those angles.

Ian: I don't like the idea that I need to live my life in accordance with someone else's writings.

Robyn: So, do you feel that religion is based on conditions?

Ian: Yes. And I think that it should come from you. In the words of Dépêche Mode..."Your own personal Jesus."

Robyn: So what is ACIM to you?

Ian: It is the best thing I've seen..."religious type" of...ah...it's a good road map.

Robyn: So, you just said that religion feels conditional to you. So does ACIM feel conditional to you?

Ian: No.

Robyn: So if religion feels "conditional" to you, then how can ACIM be religious?

Ian: Because it talks about God, Holy Spirit, and Jesus.

Robyn: See, that's where I think a lot of people over time have witnessed conditions in different types of religions, and then amongst these conditions there was God, Holy Spirit, Jesus, the disciples etc. That is what we see as religion. But at the end of the day what is the fear that...

Ian: It is mostly based on fear. Even the bible has fear-based elements.

Robyn: And then, we see God, Jesus, and Holy Spirit as "fear" because they were amongst those conditions that we came across in all those different religions. But now in ACIM, when you read "God" or "Jesus," do you ever associate it with fear?

Ian: I've never read the book.

Robyn: Yeah, but you've taken a look at parts of it.

Ian: No, I don't associate it with fear.

Robyn: And I feel like that too.

Ian: But it is difficult to view all those terms...Jesus, God etc., without associating them with what we've been taught in the past. See...but how religious was your upbringing...?

Robyn: Hey, I remember back in my twenties someone was mentioning God and I said, "Please, don't use that word, can you please use something different?" See, I felt the same.

Ian: Yeah. I think it is a common reaction.

Robyn: I think that most people do associate God with fear because of the conditions..."you must do this and you must do that." You must do all these things. It's like, you must live by the 10 commandments otherwise you are going to burn in hell.

Ian: Right.

Robyn: Well, not that it actually says that, but that is the feeling you get from it.

Ian: Yeah that *is* the feeling you get from it.

Robyn: So, of course we are going to walk away and be fearful of God.

Ian: Much of the bible is misinterpreted. There was this guy walking around two thousand years ago that was pretty smart and enlightened. And later they turned his message into, "Gotta do this, this, and this." But they got it wrong.

Robyn: Just think, it's his birthday in a few days time.

Ian: Hey, didn't they get that wrong too?

Robyn: (Chuckle) When I'm doing the Course and I come across the word "Christ," I feel different than I have ever felt with religions. It feels like a friendly book, a friendly Course. It basically says if you want to wake up here are the steps.

Ian: I think anybody that gets into the Course, before they really do that, should watch that documentary we watched. It was called "The story of A Course in Miracles."

Robyn: Yeah, that is a great documentary isn't it! They were the original people that were involved with the scribing's and publishing of the Course. Helen Schucman, Bill Thetford, Judith Skutch Whitson, and Kenneth Wapnick. And Jerry Jampolsky was in that documentary too.

Ian: Yeah. It's great.

Robyn: At the end of that documentary when Bill Thetford was at Westminster Abbey in London, I felt his energy was different, like he had changed. It was as though he was at peace. He had found something. I do recall at Gary's seminar he mentioning that Bill Thetford was talking to Judith Skutch Whitson in person one day and told her that he felt *free*. He then passed away later that day. When we saw him at the end of that documentary, it seemed as though he had found what he was looking for.

Ian: Yeah, that he was free.

Robyn: Yeah. I think that is a great documentary for people who are interested or new to the Course.

Ian: I think it is great for people that might be skeptical. The big piece for me was the fact that there were these two scientific types that weren't very religious.

Robyn: They were asking big time for the answers.

Ian: Well, Bill was the one asking. He said there has to be a better way. You know, I don't know why Helen was chosen to channel it, because Bill was the one that was really questioning it.

Robyn: Well, that is the same as Abraham-Hicks in PF1. Abraham said that Jerry Hicks was the big questioner. And if it wasn't for him then Esther Hicks couldn't channel the information because he was the one that was drawing the answers through from the powerful questioning.

Ian: Oh yeah, that's right. Watch out if I start channeling something.

Robyn: (Giggle) Yeah. But you know honey, we are all channeling every day. We are all getting answers but many just don't realize it. Every time we *receive* a word or a thought...we are being "inspired." Being "inspired" is being "in spirit."

Ian: Well, yeah, that is when we are connected.

Robyn: Yeah, that's true. So, how do you feel about the Course after you have had these religious thoughts and now you have seen me go through the lessons?

Ian: I think they are two totally separate things. The Course doesn't preach. It doesn't tell you how you should live your life. It's about a self discovery.

Robyn: Yeah, like a personal journey...

Ian: Yeah.

Robyn: I have spoken to some people who have picked up the Course and then put it down again as it wasn't feeling right or good to them at the time.

Ian: That means they are not ready. The Course is not something to be preached like religion. It's got to come from within. It's either something that is going to spark an interest or it's not. It's not something that you can preach about.

Robyn: Right. But you can set an example. And then...at the end of the day there is nobody else out there anyway. (chuckle)

Ian: What are you setting the example for?

Robyn: All I need to know is the journey that I am on. But when I know that everyone is a fragment of me, and I see someone might be...

Ian: But, you know, it's like these pioneers, these missionaries that think they have to go out and pound religion into people. They think that they have to convert them. (In Ian's controlling voice) "This will happen to you if you don't convert!"

Robyn: But if someone is lost and *looking* to find their way, then there is nothing wrong with giving or sharing something that feels right, or sharing the truth. I think that maybe it has something to do with you feeling uncomfortable in sharing this type of information.

Ian: Yeah, you are probably right.

Robyn: Maybe you are not comfortable with sharing information about the Course as you are not one hundred percent comfortable with it yourself. There are times when I have felt that way myself. But then...when your sister and husband visited you actually shared heaps with them about the Course.

Ian: Well, I felt comfortable to share it with them. They are pretty much the only ones I would share it with.

Robyn: This is how it felt to me when they came into town. It felt like you had been holding all this body of information in but you wanted to yell it out to the world. That's how it felt. It was like, they sat down, and then all of a sudden you had this right to speak out. And it felt like you kind of threw up all this stuff.

Ian: (chuckle)

Robyn: It felt that you had kept it all in. So then, why...or who cares what people think? Why wouldn't we share, if someone is asking...

Ian: Because I am still with that...hmm... (pause)

Robyn: Do you feel it may relate to a judgment you have toward the Course?

Ian: No, I have a fear of a judgment on *me*. The same as Jerry Jampolsky did back then and how he spoke of it on that documentary.

Robyn: So...if you felt entirely comfortable with the Course then you would feel like sharing the information?"
Ian: Right. And then I wouldn't feel the fear of judgment on me. Hmm...I don't know how long it took Jerry to get past that...(pause) but then I bet he wouldn't have gone on camera if he wasn't.

XMAS DAY

(Listening to Xmas carols in the background, and eating a Xmas breakfast)
Robyn: Mele Kalekemaka!
Ian: Mele Kalekemaka! Here we are, Xmas morning.
Robyn: Yes, in Punalu'u.
Ian: Drinking Mimosa's and eating from a platter of crumpets, cakes, and fruit. Mmm.
Robyn: Yeah, nice food. And a lovely Xmas morning with my honey.
Ian: Yeah. (Ian leans in for a kiss)
Robyn: (a tad teary)
Ian: What's wrong?
Robyn: I don't know. I feel like it is the end of something.
Ian: I think you might be having "a fallout" from not doing your lessons.
Robyn: Hmm, I don't know. It is kind of like the end of an era type of thing. The ending of that first year...we've gone through heaps.
Ian: Yeah.
Robyn: But it's like...it ends here in Hawaii. And it's a new beginning now when we go back. I don't know. I hope it gets easier.
(Jingle Bells is playing on the radio in the background)
Ian: I think it will.
Robyn: (sniffing) (pause) So, what do you feel we have gotten from this year?

Ian: Well, it's gone quick. We've certainly learned a lot. We've learned a lot about each other and how to deal with each other and how to deal with the ego. It's been tough.

Robyn: It's been a powerful year. Probably the most powerful and transforming year of my life.

Ian: Yeah, no doubt.

Robyn: It feels like we have been tested. Like we have been given the most precious love, and that we have been tested with it. To see if the ego can win and kill this love. When I look back at this past year that is what it feels like—it feels as though we were tested to see if we could get through it.

Ian: It does feel like a test. On one hand it feels like we have been pushed together and on the other hand it feels like we have been pulled apart at the same time.

Robyn: I wonder what will happen now that I have finished the lessons. I have heard through other students that the lessons bring up a lot to be healed. And now what will happen? Will it continue that way? Or will we find more peace now? Am I going to remember to do my forgiveness lessons? My goal every day is to remember that I am the holy Son of God and you are the holy Son of God. And everyone I come into contact with is the holy Son of God. That we are all One. It isn't easy, but that is my goal now. (pause) So...how did you feel watching me go through the lessons? How do you feel about the future now in regards to this journey?

Ian: Well, watching you go through the lessons was learning for me. I learned firsthand. I feel like I am a recipient of the benefits of doing the Course. (chuckle) That, in a sense, I went through them too, even though I haven't done them. I don't know what I am going to do now. I am just going to continue on my mental path of dealing with ego.

Robyn: So, you feel like you have gotten something from all of this?

Ian: Absolutely. I have definitely gotten something from this. I feel like a cheat though, because I haven't done the lessons. But I feel like I have gotten something from it, and I will continue doing forgiveness lessons. And I think I have a lot to sort out in my life before I do the actual lessons in the Workbook. I don't see myself going home now and doing the lessons. I mean if we were living here at this house, and we were looking out at the ocean, then I would probably run off and do a lesson.

Robyn: You feel like you would want to do them in this environment? I can understand that. It has been easier for me to do them because I have worked out of home.

Ian: And that is why I feel that it has been, well not easy, but easier for you to complete them. And fortunately you have a very loving partner who understands the Course and relates to what you are doing. (chuckle)

Robyn: (chuckle) And also, too, I feel in my heart that you and I were supposed to come together now because this was the right time for me to be doing them, and for us to be going through this. We are both strong people. We both have strong outlooks and stubborn ways, and we can test each other. That is where the ego can come through and try to destroy this love.

Ian: And we both have come from different places. I don't mean geographically either. And we have to learn about each other, as well as understand each other.

Robyn: We both have our own set of beliefs. I have my beliefs, you have yours. We have come together in our early 40's. We both haven't had, nor do we desire to have, children. So we have both given a lot of time to ourselves and had plenty of time to get to know who we each are as individuals. Now, we come together with this powerful love. But we also have to understand that we both have ego, which is very present, because we both are very sure of who we are, and what our needs are.

Ian: That is because we have both been molded over the years, and have our own individual persona's. And now we've met someone who is equally as strong with their own persona and beliefs. That is where the two waves meet.

Robyn: And now we come together, set in our ways; well, I don't know if we are so much set in our ways because we are able to understand each other. But we do both have needs that we let each other know about. Isn't that the role of the ego to have its needs met?

Ian: I don't think that is a bad thing?

Robyn: It isn't a bad thing. As long as we realize that the needs we have are the needs of the ego, and that we have opportunity to undo and heal the wrong mind.

Ian: Isn't that part of the unlearning? Because we have over these 40 odd years built up the persona that is actually based on fear and need.

Robyn: Yeah.

Ian: So, what we are doing now is unlearning what we've learned, through each other, and recognizing it in each other, and recognizing what is fear-based, or in other words, ego-based.

Robyn: Yeah. We are realizing how much of an ego base we really have.

Ian: But the problem is that when you are in the heat of that situation you have to recognize what is happening and you can't ignore it. You must acknowledge it.

Robyn: Right. Ego wants to please ego. That's the thing that traps us. And we can't just say, "Let's forgive the ego," and we are done. It is a process. It's a step by step process of undoing. It's undoing this dream. That is the point of all of this. We get hard on ourselves. We think we have to be able to do the forgiveness lessons and make all this work right now. Be healed right now. In an instant. One of the most important things I have learned this year is that we have to be able to accept the ego. It's a *process* of undoing. We have to truly learn to accept the ego and be okay with it along the way. See it for what it is and realize it isn't scary. It's just illusionary. And then continue to forgive it.

Ian: I don't think completing the lessons is like completing the Course.

Robyn: No. And maybe that is why I am teary in a sense. It is because I know that that is the end of the ignition. It's like an ignition process. I was given the key to start the motor. To start to realize what the ego is. All we are doing right now is learning how to distinguish what the ego is. What this thing is that holds us back.

Ian: And it's harder work now to stay focused on it because you don't have that little book to run back to and start doing a lesson.

Robyn: Hey, who told you it was a little book? (smiling)

Ian: I'm referring to those loose pages you carry around with you from your Workbook—which make it look like a small book smartass.

Robyn: Yes, and that's scary. In the last few days, since finishing the lessons, I feel like I'm bad because I'm not doing my lesson. It's like the ego is telling me I should be doing it.

Ian: Why would the ego tell you to do your lesson?

Robyn: Because that is the way the ego works. Isn't it the ego part of us that tells us "the should's," "the need's," and "to worry," and "to struggle." It's all part of that ego trait of saying, "You're not good enough. You should be better." That's the ego. (pause) ...Hmm, this fruit is Yummy!

Ian: I got a brand new ipod!

Robyn: And I got a brand new camera! Santa was good to us. (pause)...Look at that beautiful view out there. How can we leave that today?

Ian: We get in the car, shut the door and drive...unfortunately.

Robyn: Not that we don't like California. But there is something about Hawaii. It is so tranquil and beautiful. Ooh, there is the phone...

THE REAL DEDICATION STARTS

Ian: (later, after the phone call – still enjoying our Xmas breaky) Well, that was my sister calling from England.

Robyn: Hmm, Xmas in England today. Yesterday it was Xmas in Australia.

Ian: It seems like we have had Xmas for 2 days talking to people about it.

Robyn: Now *we* finally get Xmas! Yesterday morning we spoke to my Mum and family in Oz. Then we spoke to your Mum last night for Xmas morning in England, and we were *still* waiting for Xmas in Hawaii. We thought Santa forgot us!

Ian: We are one of the last places in the world to celebrate Xmas.

Robyn: Yeah, Santa must be tired right now...he hasn't slept for 2 days!

Ian: So, honey, I don't think you finished telling me how you feel about finishing your lessons?

Robyn: Well, I don't think I can say I have done the lessons and that's it. Now I have to ask myself, "Do I want the peace and harmony that I know I can have?" I have been shown the steps, now it is up to me to move forward and do the forgiveness lessons. It's easy to get caught in believing that dedication is only required while doing the Workbook lessons.

Ian: Yeah, that was the easy bit.

Robyn: That is where you are being guided and shown how to do the steps. Now the *real* dedication starts.

Ian: That was an interesting thing you said recently. Now that you have finished the lessons, you are asking Holy Spirit to lead you down the path. And I said, "No, I don't like that word...'lead'." I like the thought that Holy Spirit is walking *with* you hand in hand. That's the way it should be now because you have everything that you need.

Robyn: Well, it is. But it's also knowing that I need guidance as well. I sit here with you today knowing that there is work up ahead. I have finished my lessons and it doesn't mean that I can sit back and everything should magically unfold step by step. It means...dedication and awareness. Am I being aware when the ego is present? Am I dedicated enough to do the work?

Ian: That is what Ken said. If you are *aware* then that is a large part of the challenge.

Robyn: It's a huge part. And these past few days in Hawaii when you haven't felt well, I looked at that and realized that you are me, and so I needed to do a forgiveness lesson on you being sick. There is a part of me that has fear that I could still catch it too.

Ian: Well, if you *don't* catch it then that is a good testament to the Course.

Robyn: I think anything that comes up that doesn't feel comfortable requires a forgiveness lesson. When something doesn't feel good, like someone treating another person in a bad way, I have to say to myself, "Why am I witnessing this?" I am witnessing this because it is in *my* wrong mind and there is only one of us here. And if I am witnessing it then it requires healing. So when I see you are not well, I realize that is a part of me. And I realize this is a forgiveness lesson for *me*. You know, sometimes a part of me wants you to do a forgiveness lesson on *you* being sick, because I don't like seeing you sick and I don't want you to get sick again. That is where the separation comes in for me and traps me. See, I can't expect you to do a forgiveness lesson. I can't make it about *you*. But I still do. And then I separate. All I have right here and now is the ability to do a forgiveness lesson. I have to see that you are me, and realize that it is up to me to do the forgiveness lesson.

Ian: So when you started writing your book, has it gone the track you thought it would?

Robyn: No. It hasn't gone the track I thought it would. I thought I would heal more in that first year while doing the lessons. I mean I am getting insights and answers, but to go away with the information and truly live what I have learned is not so easy. You can't think a guardian angel is going to come down and carry you off. It doesn't happen that way. You must be *willing* to do the work.

Ian: So have you got the message across that you wanted to get across?

Robyn: You mean in sharing the info?

Ian: Yes.

Robyn: I think that when I began the lessons, I just felt the guidance initially to share it. I didn't know why. I didn't have an outcome. I just felt the guidance to share it.

Ian: If there is one message you could pick that you wanted to share what would it be?

Robyn: Going back on what I learned? What I take from this past year?

Ian: Yes.

Robyn: Hmm...don't assume. Don't think that everything is going to be a certain way. Be very open-minded. Allow things to come in. Allow things to come up for healing. Be ok with the ego. That is big. Be accepting that it is ALL coming up for healing. We have two choices when something comes up, we can either judge it, or we can heal it.

Ian: So do you think this book is going to give an insight to people when they are doing the Workbook?

Robyn: I think it is going to help people to realize that it's okay to screw up. It's okay to feel like the ego has a hold again. It's okay to fall in a hole because all this is coming up for healing. It is all one step ahead in the right direction. As long as we turn around and seek the lesson in healing, and work toward not judging our brother or ourselves.

(pause) So, what do you think hon? You have been there in this past year. What do you think looking back on it?

Ian: I don't think your book went the path I thought it might go. This is just my opinion — I thought you were going to give *your* opinion on the Course. And I think it has turned into more than that. I think it has turned into a very personal journey. And I think it is going to be helpful to people that are going down that path because they are going to struggle like you have done. And you don't get that comfort factor from the Course. You don't get anything that says, "It's okay if you are feeling screwed up. It's okay that you yell at somebody. It's okay that you are feeling painful emotions." You don't get that from the Course. I mean I've even heard stories of students wanting to commit suicide while doing the Course! It seems to me that this is quite an unusual and trying experience to begin to dissipate wrong mind. So I think when the reader sees a real person going through this and the emotions that surface it can be helpful. But I don't think that is initially what you planned on sharing in the book.

Robyn: I didn't have an initial plan. I followed what felt right and I really wasn't sure how it would all unfold. Prior to beginning the lessons, I had heard from other students that it gets real tough going through the lessons. But I still had no idea how it would unfold for me. I don't think anyone could pick up the 365 Workbook lessons and know what is to come. You know...looking back, prior to the Course, it is interesting how over the years you learn to deal with certain aspects of people, and you learn to let stuff go and put things under the mat. You don't want to be confrontational. Then, while doing the Workbook lessons, things come up that are out of left field. And because you want to heal, you naturally act and react differently than you would have done previous to the lessons. When we forget stuff is coming up for healing, we judge other people, and then we look at ourselves and feel guilty and say we shouldn't be reacting that way. We can sit there and judge ourselves and judge other people till the cows come home. But if we want to continue to do that...then that is where the ego wins. See, the ego was in control before, even though it didn't appear to be. It is difficult to recognize. Then, through the lessons, it is recognizable completely. And then you just go, "Wow, look at what this ego thing really is."

Ian: Yeah, that realization must come as quite a surprise.

Robyn: You know...before the Course, I understood there was ego and there was Love, and I understood the difference too, but I didn't realize just how much the ego played such a *huge* role in this experience. Right down to the seemingly happy parts of the dream—those times when we attach ourselves to the next best thing to make us feel good. It's all a *survival strategy* of the ego. So, now I have come to learn what the ego *really* is. Now I recognize it in myself and others as *multiple* false thoughts appearing real—coming from the *one* wrong mind.

Ian: I think what you have done in writing this book is give others insight into realizing what the ego really is. So that will help them to know if they want to read the book before or after.

Robyn: I didn't read the entire Course before the lessons. I read a lot of it, but not all of it. I just had a feeling to start the lessons.

Ian: No, I mean with your book. The one you are writing. Hopefully they will read that first before the lessons so they know what they are getting themselves into.

Robyn: Oh. Hey, fireworks!

Ian: Yeah. Fireworks on Xmas day. That guy has been letting fireworks off every day. It's 11 O'clock in the morning!

Robyn: Mele Kelekemaka! (pause) Hmm, you know honey, there is nobody else I could have imagined taking this journey with.

Ian: Aww. There is nobody else I could have imagined opening my eyes to this either. (kiss) Thank you baby for doing so. (pause) But we have to understand that this isn't the ending but a *new* beginning.

Robyn: Hmm, I like that. Cheers honey!

Ian: Yeah. I like it too. Cheers my little Vegemite!

We who complete Him offer thanks to Him, as He gives thanks to us. The Son is still, and in the quiet God has given him enters his home and is at peace at last.
[Manual for Teachers, pg 92, 5.5]

A special thank you to Ian for participating and sharing his views and points of interest in this book. Our journey toward waking up is a fascinating, unique, and at times, trying period. Those who enter our lives during this period offer a rare and powerful gift. It takes vulnerability and often humbling moments to walk this path toward abolishing wrong mind. It takes courage and faith. I am ever so grateful to Ian for taking a leap of faith into a land unknown, and for "sharing" this journey as a means to recognize Truth. We cannot walk this path alone. We must join with our brother to witness the Truth in our brother and ourselves.

Robyn and Ian pictured in front of Mokoli'i Island, Oahu – 8/2008

For more information or to order copies
of Robyn Busfield's books,
Forgiveness is the Home of Miracles
and *It's Time to Get Selfish,*
please visit:

www.robynbusfield.com

Printed in Great Britain
by Amazon